This book includes a combination of heart-warming, very moving and humorous stories from his own life and also some stories turned into poetry. Russ's writing is very open and about love and relationships, soul mates, family, parenting, and friendships. His kindness and love, his gratefulness, generosity and compassion shine through his writing. His stories have the "Awwww" and "wow" factor for me; some make me teary, some make me laugh out loud. A pleasure to read!

    —U. Lark

Russ Towne is a gifted soul whose honesty, pure love of life and family and his ability to see the good in all makes him a master inspiring writer. In Russ' stories that we feel his pure heart, we celebrate his triumphs, we negate the errors and we applaud the humanness in which he finds such positivity. His honor, his inspiration and his rich ability to reach down to his very soul makes us feel all warm and tingly inside. He's the brother, the father, the husband, the son and the friend who you want in your family tree. He is the golden apple of kindness, of thoughtfulness and of honesty. His stories will make you laugh, perhaps make you cry, but always keep you grateful for being alive. "Things will often get rocky, so it pays to keep rolling. That's the stone-cold truth that we never take for granite," is one of his quotes which you'll appreciate—now imagine an entire book just there waiting for you with open arms and you'll know one of my favorite authors, Russ Towne.

    —Yvonne Deane

The saying goes: "There are no atheists in a foxhole." What that means is that, when survival is what is at stake, everyone hopes God to be with them. Well, in my case, I'd rather have Russ in the foxhole with me. Russ is the kind of man you can trust with your life. Why? Because Russ is as authentic a man as you could ever hope to meet. His stories are rich with truth even though they may seem like "made up" stories. Each story is a window into how Russ sees the world and how he relates to that world with compassion and love. They can be sad, joyful but always inspiring. If you cannot meet Russ in person, I recommend that you meet him through his writing. You will not be disappointed."

  —Charlie Bedard

Heart, encouragement, forgiveness and love are themes easily picked up in the writings of Russ Towne in spite of hardships he has faced over the years. Russ teaches us that we cannot control the actions of others or the circumstances that visit us in our lives, but we can control our responses to them. If you need a little pick-me-up or if you need your faith in humanity renewed, pick up this book and read it.

  —Diana Schwenk

Reflections from the Heart of a Grateful Man

Russ Towne

Acknowledgments

Thank you to the people whose excellent work enhanced this creation:

> Gail Nelson of eBook Design, Interior Design
>
> Sandy Lardinois, Editor
>
> Shayla Eaton of Curiouser Editing, Editing of Cover Text
>
> Julie Pruitt and Gail Nelson, Cover Design
>
> Josh McGill, Illustrator/Sketches

Thank you also Norma Budden for suggesting that two of my earliest books (Reflections of a Grateful Man and From the Heart of a Grateful Man) belong together in a single volume and for suggesting the title of this book.

I'm eternally grateful.

Dedication

To my brother Roger, with deep love and respect.

Contents

I can think of no better reason to write, or to live, than to make others feel valued and special.

$$\mathcal{W}$$

What Matters to Me

*T*his is dedicated to anyone who is in the midst of struggle, heartache, pain, and grief. Dark days of any kind. And especially to those who are searching for their gifts, for the meaning of life, or even the reason they are alive.

I apologize in advance if this—or anything I write—comes across as preachy. I'm just a student of life—and a slow-learner at that—so I'm probably just about the last person on the planet who should be preaching to anyone about anything.

Anyway, you've been warned, so here goes:

I probably don't know what your gifts are, my friend, but this I do know: You have some wonderful gifts to share with the world. Gifts that it badly needs. If you haven't discovered them yet, I hope that you keep looking until you do, and when you find them, I know that you and the world will be better for it as you share them.

I can give clues to you as to where to look: The sources of your greatest pain, trauma, or sadness are often also the catalysts of one's greatest gifts for the world.

I know that life can be hard. That is easy to say. It is especially easy to say for those who haven't yet dealt with many hardships.

My father left my mother with three young children and one still in the womb when I was the oldest child and only about four years old. I nearly died of Whooping Cough as a young child, had many lung collapses, and endured two lung surgeries in my teens, got dumped by a fiancée, nearly lost my daughter to an incurable disease, suffered some business failures including one that drove me to personal bankruptcy and erased the financial resources of a lifetime of hard work, was diagnosed with Trigeminal Neuralgia (aka The Suicide Disease due to the intensity of the pain), and, most recently, My Beloved had thyroid cancer.

I share these things so you'll know that I haven't been immune to dark days and that when I say I know life can be hard, I have some idea about life not always being full of sunshine and fair winds.

But I also mention all that so I can say this: So what? Big deal. Virtually everyone has similar stories of hardship, pain, trauma, and heart-ache.

I believe that I am a better person for having experienced each of those very unpleasant things. I wouldn't wish them on anyone, but they happened. I can't change that. I can focus on what lessons I can learn from each and can have empathy for others who are going through their own tough times.

It isn't the stories that matter to me. Not mine, and not yours.

What matters to me is what I choose to do with the miracle of each new day of life. I can choose to make the most of it and enjoy and share all I can of the many blessings each day offers; or I can dwell on those sad stories and how unfair, cruel, and ugly people and life can be; or I can even squander each precious day worrying about a future that may or may not even happen, living for a tomorrow that never comes.

Like everything else in life, the choices are mine. I won't always be able to choose what happens to me and to those I love, but I WILL always be able to choose how I react to what happens, and what I do about it.

With those choices comes an amazing life-transforming power.

To make my life and my world better.

Or not.

May I choose wisely.

~~~

To give up on someone is to give up on the parts of me that I see in them.

Abyss

I know too well
What it's like
To linger
On the jagged edge
Of a deep and dark abyss.
Feel its pull.
Hear its Siren's song.
"Give up! Give in!
End my pain and shame.
No need to suffer anymore."
But even during my darkest days
When hope was but a memory
Knew even then
The abyss would lose.
That false friend
Has no chance
Against a tool I use.
Renews my hope
Helps me to endure
When all seems lost.
Make a list
All I'm grateful for.

Smile as the list grows long
The abyss loses its allure.
When I'm feeling down,
Counting blessings
Is the cure.

~~~

𝒜 dear friend named Gina shared this thought with me:

"*It is by going down into the abyss that we recover the treasures of life. Where you stumble, there lies your treasure.*"

When I've stumbled in the abyss it has often looked and felt like anything BUT treasure at the time. It has sometimes taken many years for me to realize the treasure that was there. When I finally did, I've most often discovered the treasure where my heart and spirit intersect with my wounds.

A Most Unusual Christmas Tree

*V*isitors who come to our home near the holidays are often struck by the sight of a most unusual Christmas tree. Instead of a fir or some other traditional kind, we have a palm tree decorated with Christmas lights and ornaments. It has special meaning for my family.

When our daughter was fourteen she was stricken with an "incurable" disease and nearly died. She spent about a month in the hospital, much of it in intensive care fighting for her life. She had to deal with an awful disease as well as many blood transfusions and the side-effects of the chemotherapy, steroids, and other harsh medications. She met each challenge, disappointment and setback with courage and class.

Eventually, the disease went into remission and she began to dream of having a party and a bonfire for her 16th birthday at the beach with her friends, relatives, and beloved dog Ginger. It took quite a bit of searching, but we finally found a beach that had all the necessary attributes including allowing dogs and bonfires, and that was easy to access for elderly relatives.

A week before her party, the disease flared up and 15 glorious months of remission ended.

Then, at 9 pm the night before the party, a friend called with some news that turned our plans upside down. He'd just heard that the small beach that we'd selected and the surrounding beaches were about to be overwhelmed by a 30,000-person event that would essentially close them to a private party when we'd planned to be there.

So that beach was out and no other beach within a reasonable driving distance had all of the attributes required to make her dream come true.

Our daughter had her heart set on having her family and friends, dog, and a bonfire at the beach, but as usual she didn't complain. In her young life she has had to deal with much worse things than a spoiled birthday party. But it was just the final straw on a mountain of straws that finally broke the camel's back. She sat down and quietly began to cry.

She then quickly decided that she'd rather have the party at our home so that she could at least have her dog, relatives, friends, and a bonfire. We began making the calls to invitees about the changed plans.

When guests began arriving at our home (which is about 30 miles from the nearest beach) the next day they were surprised to find a sign that read:

"Welcome to our beach, where Dogs and Bonfires are Welcome. Though the beach is small and the waves are so far away that you need to close your eyes to see them, but not the love for our daughter and her little dog too."

Laid out before them was the smallest, goofiest beach you ever saw, but it had been built with love. Our friends had at a moment's notice dreamt up creating a beach in our backyard. They had surprised us by arriving several hours earlier with a car loaded down with 660 pounds of sand, a palm tree, beach toys, fish netting, Tiki Torches and much more. Our friends and son had then helped to set everything up.

The beach was built with so much love that it quickly became real to everyone there. The birthday girl and her friends frolicked in the sand, had a barbecue, built their own huge ice cream sundaes, and splashed in the water of a little pool. Then as night fell they lit the Tiki torches and enjoyed a great bonfire.

In the dark, by the light of the torches and bonfire, and with the splashing sounds from those playing in the water of the small wading pool in the background, the scene had indeed seemed to magically transform into a beach.

That night as the girls laughed and played on the "beach" around the bonfire with our funny little dog, I felt for a moment that all was right in the world, and was very grateful to our friends for making our daughter's birthday wish come true after all.

A few months later, as the holidays neared, our daughter suggested that we use the palm tree that helped make the "beach" so special instead of getting a Christmas tree. We liked the idea so much that it is now the tree we use most every year.

Where Do Dreams Go To Die

Where do dreams go to die?
Could be an awful, terrible place.
But caterpillars become butterflies.
Drops of water become snowflakes.
Perhaps dreams are like that too
When they're crushed and all seems lost.
Maybe they become something new
Even better than what we'd sought.

There is Greatness in Goodness

There was a scene in the recent Oz movie where a man with many flaws who has wanted his whole life to be great and failed over and over again finally does something that is indeed great.

The woman he is with says something to him that is profound. It went something like this:

"Yes, you were great. But you were also something much better than that. You were good."

The longer I live, the more I have come to understand the truth and wisdom in those words.

One can be great without being good, but there is greatness in goodness.

A Five-Run Homer!

In 2012, My Beloved and I experienced a most unusual baseball game between the Giants and the Yankees. We got to see a 5-run homer, a batter run the bases backwards, and players skipping in the outfield and doing somersaults in the infield.

My wife, a Special Education teacher for Kindergartners and 1st Graders was invited by the parents of one of her students to a baseball game in a Special Education league. She invited me, and off we went on that beautiful sunny day, which featured a strong brisk breeze.

The home team was named the Giants and the Yankee's. You've probably figured out this was no ordinary game. In fact, it was a special game indeed.

All the fans cheered equally for every player of both teams. Each player was matched with a "buddy" on the field who was a Little Leaguer who volunteered to help their little buddy field or hit the ball and stay safe.

Every one of the young volunteer buddies was amazing! They stayed focused the whole game patiently guiding their little buddies in gentle, loving ways. A like number of adults would be less likely to have done nearly so well.

Speaking of adults, the grown-up volunteers, coaches, managers, and others were wonderful! They kept everyone safe while helping children who were physically, mentally, and behaviorally challenged to experience the thrill of playing baseball.

Every child got to bat every inning. There were eight players per team and the score was tied 8 to 8 at the end of the first inning, and ended in a 16 to 16 tie. It wasn't exactly a pitchers' duel, and the fielding needed some work, but their bats were on fire!

On the field were players who could barely run or hold the bat and one player in a motorized wheel chair. Boys and girls played for each team. The players went through a range of emotions during the game with smiles dominating, but frustration and tears, too. There were show-boats and shy players, and some who got overwhelmed by it all. And, you couldn't ask for a better announcer or fans. It was a wonderful way to spend part of the day.

To say I was touched by it all would be an understatement. My eyes puddled up several times during the game as I saw people being beautiful toward each other. It must have been the brisk breeze blowing dust into my eyes.

Yeah, that must have been it ...

Abled

I've often found that "disabled" people are some of the most "abled" people I know. I've learned much about living and life from people who have been labeled disabled.

I'll bet many of you have found the same.

I now often make eye contact, smile, and say hello to people who are labeled disabled, and if the situation permits, I talk with them if they appear to welcome it.

~~~

Kindness on the Mind

*W*hen one has kindness on the mind, the world can't help but be a more beautiful place.

Overcome to Become

I just completed a comment on a friend's blog with this sentence:

"I'm all-the-more proud of her because of what she has had to overcome to become who she is."

I was referring to My Beloved but as I pushed the send button I realized that is true about many of the people I know. I factor in how much they've had to overcome to become the people they are today.

Some people start the race of life with the huge weights of poverty, illiteracy, physical disabilities or deformities, mental or other illness, emotional roadblocks, abuse, addictions, depression, terrible modeling by their parents, or no parents from early after their birth, and more.

I try to remind myself of their backstory. Sometimes someone might appear not to have come far in their lives until I've learned what they had to overcome to get there.

The world is full of back stories. We all have them. I wonder how much better I would treat everyone if only I knew the burdens they carried. When I am wise enough to think of such things, my words, thoughts, and actions grow kinder, and I become more patient, compassionate, understanding, and forgiving.

In other words, I become closer to the person I'm focused on becoming.

Lesson-Rich Windstorms

$\mathcal{A}$ lot of people are going through some very challenging (I like to think of them as "lesson-rich") times right now.

If windstorms are howling all around you, may they soon expose even more of the beauty of your spirit.

One great thing about windstorms—even the fiercest—is that sooner or later they blow over.

Anchor yourself to your spirit and nothing can blow you away. It can keep your feet on the ground when the winds are howling, give you wings to soar when gentle breezes return, light your way in the darkness, warm you when the world seems so cold, and help you to connect with others in wonderfully deep and powerful ways.

~~~

$\mathcal{I}$ believe it is often from a person's greatest pain that their greatest gifts and strengths are forged.

Some Gifts I'd Love to Return

My last comments where I said tough times are "lesson-rich" may have come across as glib. It wasn't meant to be. While I believe challenging times are indeed lesson-rich and hold gifts for us, there are quite frankly some gifts I would have loved to return.

As I mentioned earlier my family has faced some major health and financial challenges in recent years.

Each was a lesson-rich gift. But those gifts came with pain, fear, despair, and grief.

As each of those challenges were happening, I'd have gladly returned those "lesson-rich gifts" or exchanged them for an end of the pain, fear, despair, and grief.

But as my family and I survived each of these difficulties, we grew stronger, more confident that we can face whatever life throws at (err, I mean "offers to") us. We are better people for having gone through such times.

And I'd be perfectly happy not receiving any more such lesson-rich gifts.

Sweet Elixirs and Bitter Brews

I've learned that it is wise to enjoy every drop of the delicious juice of the good times because sooner or later I'll be drinking a very bitter brew indeed.

I've learned that the great phrase "this too shall pass" works both ways.

For those drinking the bitter brew right now, may the sweetness of kindness and compassion from others—and from yourself—help to make the experience more palatable until you taste the sweet elixirs of life once again.

Need's Answered Call

Love in action
A beautiful sight
My whole heart smiles
The world feels right.
Kindness and connection
Make my spirit glow
My joy so great
Tears overflow.
Feel so grateful
For need's answered call
Blessed to be alive
And part of it all.

Great Spirits

I have great respect and admiration for people who have experienced the worst kinds of hell on earth but do not succumb to doing evil or doing nothing. People whose spirit is so great they help their fellow humans even in the worst situations.

Survivors of the Holocaust, wretched prison camps, and terrible wars, sometimes describe such great spirits; those who give their last morsel of food so that another might live, or risk severe beatings or death to get medicine for another who is sick, or literally give the shirt off their back to save another from brutal cold.

I'm grateful for the stories I hear about them because they warm my heart and fill it with hope.

As long as their stories keep being told, those heroes will still live in the hearts of all who appreciate such greatness of spirit, along with the generations of others who are descendants of those saved by such wonderful spirits—literally a living legacy that may endure and grow for centuries.

~~~

Speaking from your heart inspires others to do the same. It helps others to feel connected, important, and loved. Whatever you do, if you do it with love, is important and needed. The world can always use more love, kindness, and compassion.

A Warm Heart on a Cold Day

*F*rom the time I was a young boy through most of my thirties, I tended not to fit in with most of my peers. I was introverted, socially awkward, lacked confidence, and often felt shunned and ridiculed by my peers, classmates, and co-workers.

This often made interacting with people painful.

I often played alone in my room and dreaded most group activities.

Some of those shadows remain to this day, though as I have changed, the sunlight-to-shadow ratio has improved immensely. But I still reflexively find myself hesitating to do things in groups even when I know the group loves me.

I've learned that shadows almost never completely go away, and can negatively impact my attitude, life, and decisions, but the light of understanding, compassion, kindness, forgiveness, and gratitude—for everyone including myself—is the best antidote for, and protection against, even my darkest shadows.

When I was probably about 9 or 10 years old, I accepted an invitation to go on a trip to the mountains to play in the snow with a large group of children, most of whom I didn't know. I was one of the smallest and youngest. The older kids taunted and teased, and then shunned me. I was lonely and feeling bad about myself and angry at the others.

To make matters worse, I was very scrawny (people described me as gaunt). I was a city kid who lived in a temperate climate and wasn't used to snow or cold weather. I came from a family of seven. We couldn't afford fancy snow gear—or any snow gear for that matter.

For example, I didn't have water and snow-repellent shoes or overshoes. I think I only had three pairs of shoes: "sneakers," dress shoes, and slippers. So I went with the sneakers.

Before I left for the trip, mom tried to help me keep my feet warm and dry by having me wear two pairs of cotton socks—we didn't have wool or thick cold-weather socks—and she gave to me some thin plastic bread wrappers to put over the socks before I put my shoes on to try to keep my feet and socks from getting soaked. She did her best with what she had.

Unfortunately, between my complete lack of body fat and of not being conditioned to cold weather, and with the outfit I had on that not only didn't help me stay dry or warm but did invite ridicule from the older boys, I was very quickly wracked with uncontrollable full-body shivering and felt absolutely miserable and alone on a snowy hilltop crowded with people having fun.

At the bottom of the snow hill a parent volunteer had opened the tailgate of his station wagon and made a big pot of cocoa for us. He was a stranger to me. I shook like a leaf in a windstorm as I stumbled over to him for some hot chocolate. I must have been a picture of abject misery.

He handed a cup of the steaming elixir with the wonderful aroma to me. I thanked him and began to turn away. He said,

"Excuse me son." I turned back toward him, concerned that maybe I'd done something wrong. He continued in a kind voice, "I've noticed that you are always so polite. Many boys aren't. I appreciate that you are. Thank you."

It was a simple acknowledgement, but at that moment, it meant the world to me. Where there had only been freezing coldness a moment before, this kind stranger had brought warmth. And remarkably, even now as I remember his kindness 45 years later, it still warms my heart.

Thank you to that wonderful person and to everyone who brings kindness and a smile to those badly in need of both. My world is a brighter place with you in it.

I am Here

Your sorrow shows in your eyes and on your careworn face
They reflect a weary spirit that's in a painful place
The smiling mask you wear when you say everything's OK
Can't hide from me the tragedy you still suffer from today

I can see and feel such things because I've been there before
When dreams give way to nightmares and sleep's not safe anymore
I can sense your exhaustion from those long and lonely nights
When darkness lasts forever and you pray for morning light

But I see you're a survivor and surrender's not your way
I know the courage it can take just to face another day
I know too well how horrible some things in life can be
And the cost of all you've lost so devastatingly

I'll help you find forgiveness for those who did you wrong
So you can purge the pain and hurt that's festered for too long
Poison from a wound so deep it's slowly killing you
I know the symptoms all too well because I've had them too

From all your grief and torment I'll help you find release
For you deserve a life of joy and greater inner peace
I'll hold you tight in my arms and whisper in your ear,
"You are safe, you are loved, with all my heart I am here."

Mr. Rogers

One of my heroes is Fred Rogers (also known as Mr. Rogers on his children's television show). It wasn't that he was a celebrity. They are a dime a dozen in today's world. I probably only watched a total of 15-30 minutes combined of his episodes as I was channel surfing. I knew very little of him when his show was on. From his television persona, I thought he probably was a gentle man, but perhaps a little weird.

A few years ago my middle son Brian sent an audio book to me that he had just read about Mr. Rogers with a strong recommendation to listen to it. I thought I'd be bored based on the subject matter but gave it a try.

Instead, I became fascinated by the man, his kindness, compassion, goodness, and his vision and mission regarding communicating with children in ways that help them to deal with their fears, questions, insecurities, curiosity, etc. He spoke to them as a trusted friend.

He didn't care how many adults made fun of him. He was even made fun of on Saturday Night Live. That didn't matter to him. The children of the world did. He loved them and they loved him.

I more recently learned that he came out of retirement shortly after September 11, 2001 happened and made a special show to talk to the children and help them work through what they had heard and what they were feeling about the events and reactions of that tragic and fateful day.

I wish he was here to do the same after recent tragedies.

I didn't know him, but I miss his presence in our world. I would have liked to have been his friend and would have been proud to have called him a friend of mine.

~~~

I believe that happiness is not a matter of what happens in my life. It's a matter of what's happening in my heart.

The Threshold of Your Heart

I read a quote attributed to Khalil Gibran that said, "The teacher who is indeed wise does not bid you to enter the house of his wisdom but rather leads you to the threshold of your mind."

I believe that the best teachers also lead to the threshold of your heart and inspire you to enter.

~~~

Where My Heart Leads

I saw a humorous photo that showed two signs on the same pole:

The top one read: "One Way"

The one bottom one read, "Good luck figuring out which one."

Which way? To me that is simple (but not always easy): I follow where my heart leads.

The Beauty Within

𝒜 young person who is dear to me recently made comments about herself suggesting that she thought she wasn't pretty.

May she truly understand the truth in my reply to her:

"I wish that you could see the beauty within you that I see when I look at you. You are beautiful on the outside, too, but to me, one's internal beauty is far more radiant and important than mere external beauty. I wish a mirror could be invented that would allow you to see your internal beauty, for if you did, you'd see the goodness and greatness within you."

~~~

The Beauty of Your Spirit

The beauty of your spirit
Radiates all over you
I only wish that you could see
Your beauty as I do

The Secret Places

*M*ay your adventure take you to many places and, best of all, to the secret places in your heart and spirit that ache to be discovered.

~~~

That is Who You Are

A close friend and I kid each other a lot because, in many ways, we are very different (though in key ways that truly matter we are very much the same—although he'd never admit it!) ;-D!

One day he made a comment that deeply resonated within me and helped me to adjust the way I look at myself.

As he was kidding me about a sweet song I'd written, he added, "You might as well stop fighting it; that is who you are."

"That is who you are." Yup. It's who I am. Once I surrendered to that very basic notion, my life started to click even better into place.

May you know who you are or recognize it sooner than I did.

This wondrous learning adventure called life continues …

Downright Inconvenient

$\mathcal{A}$ man who recently learned of a life-threatening health condition for his dog was listening to a song I co-wrote called "My Old Friend" while at work and experienced some emotions in a fairly open (not a lot of walls and privacy) environment. (For most men in the U.S., being seen showing sentimentality or certain emotions is often a source of embarrassment. It is for me, too. I believe that we're culturally wired and conditioned to feel that way.)

I was pleased that the man trusted me enough to be able to share that experience with me. I said that as a songwriter, it is a wonderful compliment to hear that a song touched someone in such a deep way. I added that my emotions also show at times I sometimes wish they didn't.

It was then that a revelation occurred:

Perhaps he and I (and folks like us) are the lucky ones. We feel our feelings so profoundly that they manifest in ways that we can't hide even when we want to. I'd rather have to deal with such situations than be unfeeling or not in touch with my emotions.

Of course, the middle ground would very be nice, too: Feeling deep feelings and being able to not let them show most of the time. I believe that most men—and probably a lot of women too—fall into this category.

There are times when it is downright inconvenient, and other

29

things, to walk around blurry-eyed after being deeply touched by a beautiful scene, song, or other experience.

But all things considered, there is a part of me that is glad I do. I wouldn't be who I am if I didn't.

A Model of the Type of Person I Aspire to Be

I'm a lighthouse lover. To me they symbolize many positive things including quiet strength, service, sacrifice for the good of others, a beacon of hope, rising above challenges, a friend reaching out to help, standing up for those in trouble, competence and confidence, a safe haven, steadfastness, reliability and responsibility, being able to stand up to and get through life's mightiest storms, and more. In short, they model the type of person I aspire to be.

Seeing Things as We Are

1 believe it was Anais Nin who said, "We don't see things as they are, we see them as we are." If that is true—and I believe it is—then it seems to me that if I want to experience more good things, it pays to keep seeking and sharing whatever good things I can find in myself and others.

~~~

1'm a slow learner in this adventure called life but even I have picked up some precious gems of wisdom along the way. Here are some of them:

The best way to surround myself with supportive, kind, loving people is by being supportive, kind, and loving.

Finding my own creative voice and sharing it is a path of joy and growth for me.

No matter how good or bad something is there will always be people who like it and those who don't.

If something is from one's heart, it's beautiful.

If I'm having fun, I've already won.

Right Now

I believe that many incredible people and things are all around us every day if we take the time with an open mind and eyes and look closely enough to see them.

Snowflakes. Flowers. Neighbors. Stars. A drop of water. A grain of sand. Love. Babies. Sunsets.

Strangers who could become the best of friends.

Some who'd even risk their lives to save ours without even knowing us.

Incredible. Truly extraordinary. Right now. Where we live and around the world.

When I see life and the world in this way, I feel a great sense of connectedness and gratitude.

Money for a Taxi Ride

My Beloved and I were out on the town with some other couples when an elderly woman who appeared quite down on her luck and perhaps homeless walked up to our group and asked if we were going in a specific direction. We said we were. She asked if we could perhaps give a lift to her because she had someplace important to be and had no car or money.

As we had driven together, the owner of the car said, "Sorry, our car is too small and we can't help you." Then he walked away.

When no one was looking, another member of our group took some money from his wallet and dropped it on the ground. He then bent down to pick it up and handed it to the elderly lady. As he did so, he said, "I think you may have dropped this ma'am. It should be enough to hire a taxi to take you to where you want to go."

The elderly woman's eyes misted over with happiness and surprise as she took the money. She gave a knowing and grateful look to him as she thanked him.

I'll never forget the feeling I had when I saw the look in the woman's eyes.

Those eyes reminded me once again how small kindnesses can make huge differences in the lives of others.

It brightened my evening and lifted my spirit to witness such love in action.

The Worst Kind of Loneliness

Most people have been touched by the tragedy of suicide. That saddens me for the person and for the world that is deprived of their gifts.

I don't know what the total answer to that tragedy is, but I'll bet it involves kindness and reaching out to those whose desperation and loneliness eat away at their spirit like a corrosive acid until there is so little left of their spirit that they can no longer even feel it.

That has got to be the worst kind of loneliness when even hope and faith feel like false friends.

But kindness is an acid remover. It helps the spirit to shine and grow and reveal itself to the person to whom kindness is shown and to the person being kind.

Kindness offers to each of us the incredibly powerful ability to help transform lives and perhaps even save them.

We may not be able to save every life, but every life saved offers greater hope for humanity.

A Simple Act

*W*hen I was in my late teens I thought I was having a heart attack, but it proved to be a collapsed lung instead. The doctors said the lung might heal itself. It didn't.

It was like a balloon with a slow leak. The air—my AIR—would leave the lung and get stuck between the outside of my lung and inside of my chest cavity. It hurt.

I was scared. It got to the point after multiple collapses that I couldn't walk across a level parking lot without stopping to gasp for air.

Then, the unthinkable happened. My other lung started going bad. I knew that if they both deflated at the same time I would die, even if I was in the hospital on an operating room table.

It was also about then that my fiancée at the time—not the woman who later became my wife—decided she loved another man more than me and broke off our engagement.

And, my oldest and closest friend had just moved to Iowa.

I was lonely, heart-broken, lung-broken, in pain, with an unknown future, facing (if I lived long enough) two dangerous and very painful surgeries.

I didn't care if I lived or died, and I was leaning in the direction that would permanently take all my pain away.

As I understand it, each surgery required that my ribs be

separated far enough apart that a total of three hands could work inside me at the same time. All I know is that, when I came out of the surgery, I had about an 18-inch scar running up my back from one of my sides, and a LOT of stitches. Pain does not come close to describing what I felt. Agony was closer, but perhaps even it doesn't do justice to what I was experiencing.

I think I was in ICU for about a week and began recovering from home for three more weeks before heading back for my second surgery. When it was done, I had about 36 inches of scars and stitches, and even more pain. While I was in the hospital the second time, there was no position I could be in that didn't involve lying on stitches and/or vital tubing, and incredible pain.

Just about the point at which I didn't think things could become worse, they did.

A nurse turned me on my side that had just been operated on so that I was lying on my wound, stitches, and newly separated ribs. Despite my strong protests, she propped me up and wedged me in so that I couldn't move. Then she ignored me and my whispered pleas for the rest of her shift. I was in so much pain and had so little lung capacity that whispering was the best I could do. I was reduced to whimpering and tears.

Then an angel of mercy arrived in the form of a young male nurse in an era when that was still somewhat of a rarity. He took one look at me, and a look of compassion came over him as he immediately helped get me into a less painful position.

It might have been a simple act of mercy and kindness for him—

one that he probably forgot soon later—but his kind act remains warm in my memory and heart three and a half decades later.

To that wonderful nurse, and all others like him, thank you for all you do to help ease pain and suffering, and for making my world a better place.

~~~

Peace begins not with a mob but with a lone and scared person who listens to their heart.

Courage Comes In All Sizes

*B*ecause this story happened about twenty years ago it is likely that some of the "facts" I seem to recall have likely been blurred by the mists of time. Any inaccuracies are unintentional.

I'd come across an article in our local newspaper about a mother of two young children who had done something quite extraordinary. I don't remember her name and I didn't save the newspaper article so I'll call her "Mary."

She was alone in her car when she came to an accident scene. An armored truck had overturned, trapping a guard inside as gasoline leaked onto the street. The thick metal door on the side of the truck that would have enabled him to escape was now out of reach above him and too heavy to lift from beneath.

A lot of money had spilled out the back of the truck onto the pavement. A crowd of people had gathered. Instead of trying to help the trapped crew, they started scooping up the money for themselves.

As a single mother with two young children, the money must have looked mighty tempting to Mary, but rather than join the mob and take some of the money for herself, she risked her life by climbing atop the truck as it lay on its side. She tried to lift the door to let the guard out but it was too heavy.

Mary yelled to the mob, asking for help and telling them the money wasn't theirs and that they shouldn't be taking it. Everyone ignored her and just kept grabbing the money.

As the gas continued leaking and pooled all around the truck, Mary knew that a single spark could engulf the truck and everyone near it in flames. Still, she stayed on the truck and continued struggling with the door.

Mary was not a large woman and she was fighting gravity and the full weight of the door. It took all her strength, but she was finally able to open it a crack. Just as she thought things were starting to improve, they suddenly got much worse.

The guard inside saw the door being opened and thought he was about to be robbed. He drew his gun and aimed it at her. As Mary finally wrestled the door all the way open she stared straight into the muzzle of his gun!

Tense moments ticked by. Finally Mary was able to convince the guard that she was just trying to set him free. He cautiously put his gun away and she helped him climb out of his heavy metal cage.

Mary and the guard quickly began gathering up the money to try to keep it from the mob.

The police eventually arrived and the mob scattered.

The article went on to say the tow truck company sent two dozen roses to thank Mary for what she had done.

I was surprised and disappointed that, considering all Mary had risked and done for the armored car company, they just gave her two dozen roses. The more I thought about it, the more I became determined to fix what I thought had been an injustice.

We were a struggling one-income family back then and didn't have much money, but My Beloved agreed to the idea of trying to find a way to anonymously send a substantial monetary reward to Mary.

We thought the best way to do that would probably be to contact the newspaper so I left a message for the reporter who'd written the article. He promptly called me back and I explained what we had in mind and the reasons behind the idea. He asked if it would be OK if he mentioned our names in an article and I reiterated that we wanted to remain anonymous, but that it would be OK if he mentioned that Mary got a reward from anonymous donors. I asked him if he would either send the money to her or ask her for permission to give her address to us so we could. He said he'd call her and let us know what she said.

A while later, the reporter called to say that Mary had made a counter-proposal. She didn't want to accept the money unless she could meet the donors and thank us personally.

When My Beloved heard Mary's request, she suggested that we invite her and her two young children to dinner. What a great idea! It was a way to further honor Mary, and for her children to see that their mom was being honored for what she had done.

An added bonus is that our young children could meet Mary and see first-hand that a hero looks like an ordinary person, and what makes a person a hero is that they do what needs to be done, regardless of the consequences.

My Beloved and I looked forward to meeting Mary, too, but if we'd have known what was going to happen that evening, we might have canceled the whole thing. I am embarrassed about it and very rarely mention what happened to anyone.

I called the phone number that the reporter had given to me

and spoke to Mary, giving her directions to our house.

I believe these were the days before the average person had cell phones or GPS. I mention this because it helps to explain what happened next, though, in truth, the primary reason for the disaster was that I can sometimes be a complete idiot.

The night the meeting was scheduled, My Beloved was busy making the dinner. I don't remember what it was, but it was one of those that should be served shortly after cooking, and doesn't stay warm well for long.

If I recall correctly, we got a call from Mary a little after her scheduled arrival time. She had been following my directions and was now far away from our neighborhood. Mary told me where she was, and I gave her directions to get back to a street that was part of the original directions. I told her and my wife that Mary should be here in about fifteen minutes.

My Beloved looked at her dinner with a nervous look in her eyes. Fifteen minutes later, no Mary, and the dinner was looking well past its prime.

A while after that I got another call from Mary, she was again far from our neighborhood and again, I verbally steered her to the original directions I'd given to her. By now, Mary was probably wondering if this was all somehow a cruel practical joke. My Beloved looked at the dinner with hopeless eyes.

About fifteen minutes later, Mary called again and this time asked me if I'd go through all the directions all over again. I did, but this time included a critical street that I'd apparently forgotten to mention in my original call to her. OOPS!

By now, I had two very frustrated women, four very hungry children, and a very embarrassed self to deal with. My Beloved looked at the disaster that her dinner had become with disgust, and probably gave the same look to me then, too, but as I said earlier, certain things may have been blurred by the mists of time.

At long last, Mary and her two young children arrived. I apologized every way I knew how and Mary graciously accepted them. My Beloved then apologized for the ruined dinner and Mary graciously accepted her apologies and did her best to eat a dinner that was barely recognizable as food.

The rest of the evening THANKFULLY went well. I remember Mary as being young, friendly, and relatively short in height—very different than I pictured her from the newspaper article. Her young children were cute and very well behaved. We learned a bit about each other, the kind of jobs we had, etc.

My wife and I then presented her with an envelope with the money in it. As we did so, we told her in front of her children and ours that we were honored to have her at our home and that she was a hero in our eyes.

I hope that memory remains with all the children throughout their lives.

Mary, wherever you are, thank you again for the choices you made and the risks you took on that scary day at the overturned armored truck, for forgiving me for the terrible directions and the ruined dinner, for honoring our home with your presence, and for being a model of courage and humility to our children.

This Gratitude Thing

I believe the recipe for lasting happiness may be a bit different for various people, but I'll bet that, for everyone, it involves heaping helpings of gratitude.

I don't know any happy people who aren't grateful. There must be something to this gratitude thing.

I watch for evidence of the spirit in others. As I developed the habit to do so, I began to notice that it is everywhere—and I love how my spirit responds to experiencing the spirit in others. It is a wonderfully self-reinforcing cycle.

~~~

A Different Kind of GPS

*M*any people rely on GPS to find their way. I believe that whether one is in park or flying down the road of life, relying on another form of GPS is wise: "Goodness Plus Spirit" (aka your heart.)

The Most Selfish Thing I've Ever Done

I carried anger and bitterness for much of my life. In some cases I noticed that the people who had done things that led to those feelings—and refused to even acknowledge what they'd done—had gotten on with their lives while I was still mired in pain and worse.

Over time, I began to realize how much my feelings of hurt, anger, resentment, and bitterness were hurting me while not hurting them in any way. In some cases, they may not have thought about me for a long time.

So, I did a hugely selfish thing. I forgave them. I refused to let their old actions have control over me anymore. I did it completely for myself. I kept focusing on myself and my needs rather than on their actions. I made it all about me.

Eventually, I was able to begin healing. Amazingly, at some point, I even began to notice that I'd become a better person as a result.

Later still, I began to appreciate the "bad" events and betrayals, the lies and deceptions, for who and what the situations had helped me to become.

Stronger. More empathetic. Wiser. Kinder.

Those were MY choices and MY actions, and I was proud for having made and taken them.

I didn't stop trusting people less, but myself more. I worked on myself and focused on what I wanted most in my life.

At the top of my list were people who love, trust, and appreciate me for who I am. I had a lot of work to do on myself, but it got easier. Over time, my relationships and world transformed into something beautiful and magnificent from one that had been lonely, dark, and cold.

I have much respect and empathy for anyone who struggles to forgive. I know it can be a big—sometimes huge—challenge, but I wish everyone who is in that place great success.

If you are hurting, I don't know who hurt you or how badly, but I do know that I and many, many others wish good things for you, easing of your pain, and healing.

May you find what you seek and get what you need.

Collateral Compassion and Kindness

I rarely feel anger for more than a few seconds or minutes, and hate is an emotion I thankfully purged from myself long ago for completely selfish reasons.

But when I feel disappointment, it typically turns to understanding and then compassion (and sometimes even love on my better days) when I take the time to learn the whole story behind a person's actions or situation.

I do these things for myself because my life and my world are made better when I do them. If, in the process, others receive collateral compassion and kindness, I'm gladdened by it.

~~~

I believe that the extent to which you admire goodness and beauty in others, is a direct reflection of the beauty and goodness within you.

A Beautiful Choice

Ugly is in the mind of the beholder
The heart is where beauty is found
Why focus on the ugly
When beauty is all around?

~~~

G etting back up after falling is a critical first step and keeps one in the game, but, to me, it is what one does after they are back up that often makes all the difference.

The Inner Frontier

The inner frontier can sometimes be a scary place, but that is where I found most of the sweetest juice, wisdom, and growth that life has to offer.

~~~

Weird Isn't So Weird After All!

I lived much of my life in great fear. Fear of rejection. Fear of making a fool of myself. Fear of being different or weird.

Now I know that everyone is different and in some ways weird. And if everyone is weird, then weird is probably not so weird after all! ;-D! Isn't that weird?

When the discomfort of not sharing myself with the world became greater than my fear of doing so, I finally began to let the world see who I am. And to the world's great credit, and my great relief and gratitude, it reacted to who I am much better than I ever dreamed possible. Thank you, World!

The Treasure

There are pieces of my spirit
In all that I create
Offers of connectedness
I hope will resonate

May you find what I write
To be loving, kind, and true
Inspiring a deeper delving
Into the treasure that is you

May these bridges of love
Remind all my sisters and brothers
Of the greatness and the goodness
Within yourselves and others

Love in Action

$\mathcal{A}$ friend named Bill once told me that he thinks kindness is love in action.

I agree. It is now one of my favorite sayings.

I believe there is much truth and wisdom in those five words.

That helps explain to me why I focus so much on kindness; the kindness of others and kindness I can show toward others.

Actions do indeed speak louder than words.

My Journey to Forgiveness

*T*here were times when I carried anger, bitterness, and even hatred. I slowly began to realize that they were too heavy a burden to bear, and were consuming and destroying my life and future. I finally understood that down to my core and realized I had a choice.

Wishing was not good enough. Neither was false forgiveness, nor the "I want to forgive but I can't" approach. I'd been stuck in such places until I realized I was only hurting myself, and that only true forgiveness, and moving on, would enable me to break free from the internal chains and prisons that I'd created for myself.

I decided that I wanted to be happy and FREE of the terrible burdens of hatred, bitterness, and anger, more than I wanted and needed to CLING to my hatred, bitterness, and anger.

I'd kept victimizing myself by running the same old stories over and over in my head and acting the part of the victim long after the perpetrators had moved on (and probably forgotten all about me in some cases.)

I chose to stop being a "victim" and start being a survivor. That mind set helped a lot. It helped me to do one of the most wonderful things I've ever done FOR MYSELF. I forgave. Truly forgave. I found the gifts that each situation had given to me. Sometimes it took a long time to find or recognize them, but they were always there.

While my hatred and bitterness are gone (and hopefully will

never return!), I still sometimes briefly get angry at the actions, attitudes, or words, of myself or others.

I'm not anger-free, just mostly anger-free. But the bouts of anger rarely last more than a few seconds or minutes.

I'm still a work in progress, but considering where I started, I feel great about how far I've come.

~~~

The answers were inside me all along, covered up by painful memories. I had to work through my fear and pain to begin to see that my greatest gifts for sharing with the world were there and aching to be freed.

Collateral Kindness

I was once asked what I put on my cornflakes or breakfast bars in the morning that always made me so cheerful. Reading her comment warmed my heart and made me laugh, because I'm far more of a Night Owl than a Morning Glory by nature. I can be downright grumpy when I wake up.

But, my life is so filled with blessings that I should awaken with a beaming smile and tap-dance to work.

I've done some things to reduce the grumps. I've found that getting eight hours of sleep helps my disposition a LOT, and I've noticed that, if I have a lot of sugar, I tend to feel depressed shortly afterward, so I'm beginning to eat less of it, especially in the morning.

As for my cheerful writing, my day is brighter when I focus on positive, upbeat, uplifting things, so I selfishly write about things that brighten my day.

If my writing also brightens your day and those of others, I guess the collateral kindness simply can't be helped. ;-D!

Being There

$\mathcal{M}$any of the most powerful moments in my life, the times I feel the most alive, the most useful, and the most connected to everyone and everything, are those times I am there when someone needs me the most.

Just being there and walking through the fire or sitting in it with them, creating a safe space for their anger, grief, despair, pain, shame, loneliness, fear, and/or whatever else they are experiencing or being tormented by, and staying with them until the fire subsides, has often meant everything to me.

People often thank me for being there for them as though they somehow owed a debt of gratitude to me for being there for them. From my perspective, it is I who owe them, for the huge gift they gave to me for allowing me to be with them in their most awful moments, sharing their darkest hours, worst fears, and most painful times.

I live for such moments. It is why I'm alive. I've arranged my life so that I can drop everything and be there—any time of the day or night.

To those who have honored me by allowing me to be there at such times, I owe a debt of gratitude. Thank you!

The Beauty Within

*G*reat sculptors can see the beautiful form within a block of granite.

It is also possible to see, feel, and experience the beautiful spirit of others regardless of what they look or act like on the outside, and often even before they realize the beauty within themselves.

~~~

I would be unlikely to bet against anyone once their actions, words, vision, heart, and spirit became aligned, no matter how many prior failures they experienced.

Falling Down

When one falls down again and again
Getting back up is an important start
But it's what one does when they do
That's a better measure of their heart!

Tears

This is dedicated to all who are in pain, feeling alone, broken-hearted, and/or grieving—or have been. In other words, this is dedicated to everyone.

Part of being alive is experiencing pain. For many people, pain can lead to tears, and for some, tears pile shame onto their pain.

I believe that tears can be a sign and source of strength, of connectedness, of being able to truly feel when so much of the world does all they can to get and stay numb.

Tears are a way of acknowledging that I can STILL feel. I can feel my pain. I can feel yours. I haven't given up on myself, on you, or on the world. I'm strong enough to hang in there despite the pain and the desire to numb it.

The tears are here to not only help heal but to enlighten—to literally lighten our load and illuminate a life lesson that must be learned so growth can occur; to help us become wiser and stronger. And, in the process, to gain the courage to forgive and to show kindness and have empathy not only to friends, nor just to strangers, but to all who may have wronged or harmed us.

If tears are from pain today, they are a gift. Embracing them can lead to healing and help us grow stronger. While it may or may not feel like it at the time, I believe that every tear is a step away from pain and toward the possibilities of greater joy in our lives.

I know that someday more tears will come—for you and for me—because life offers many detours and obstacles from which we may learn and grow.

If we are patient, and if we continue to work on making ourselves the kind of people we so badly want to become, life will someday provide us with a very different kind of tears—tears of joy. And those are worth every step and every painful tear that brought us to a more joyous life.

Until that day, please know that there are many in the world—most who have never had the opportunity to meet you—who wish good things for you.

I am one of them.

That Which Lies Within

I read somewhere recently that life isn't about finding yourself, it's about creating yourself. While I like that saying and believe that is certainly true on some levels, I also believe that life is very much about finding one's true self: That pure spirit that is beneath all the layers of self-doubt, pain, fear, shadows, negative labels, and other very real but harmful things that keep a person's spirit buried in darkness.

I believe that the spirit inside everyone is so powerful that even a single one can change the world.

Some spirits shine in very public ways and are well-known throughout the world.

Many spirits shine quietly or even anonymously, bringing their light, love, smiles, compassion, kindness, and warmth to others who are struggling in the darkness of despair, grief, loneliness, pain, suffering, and poverty.

As for poverty, I've learned that there are even worse kinds than being without money—the kinds where people have no hope, no faith, and receive no human kindness—not even a gentle touch or a loving hug—and those who feel worthless.

I don't believe the word "worthless" does the feeling justice. People who feel that way don't just feel worth LESS, they feel like they are worth NOTHING.

When we discover or rediscover the spirit within ourselves, we can share its light, love, and warmth with others. Sometimes in that sharing—like one candle lighting another—we can help someone who is scared and stumbling in the darkness of their shadows to begin to see glimpses of the beauty of their own spirit.

Every time a candle is lit or a spirit is re-kindled, our world gets a little bit brighter and warmer. For the person who experiences their spirit for the first time or re-experiences it after a long while, their world isn't just a bit brighter and warmer.

It can be an awakening to the love and beauty inside and all around them that changes and enhances their life and attitude forever.

It can mean the difference between life and death, merely existing versus truly living, hiding in fear or confidently making their future and our world much brighter.

Add Extra to Ordinary

I was headed out the door to meet with a new investment client when the headline for an ad in an open magazine caught my eye:

"Add Extra To Ordinary"

What an extraordinary tag line! (It was for Bertoli Olive Oil by the way.)

"Add Extra To Ordinary" Those four words stayed with me, and as I drove to my appointment, I realized how powerful and universal that message is. Every aspect of life can be made better if we take the time to "Add extra to ordinary."

So often even a little extra effort, a little extra thoughtfulness, a little extra kindness, a little extra enthusiasm, and a little extra caring can make a huge difference in our own lives and the lives of others.

I've even experienced first-hand how a little extra effort has saved lives. There are few better feelings in the world than to hear someone say:

"You may not know it, but what you did that night saved my life!"

All I'd done was be there for a friend. A simple act that didn't even take much time and very little extra effort. But that extra effort not only changed a life, it saved one.

I hadn't even been aware at the time that a life hung in the balance and would have been lost if I hadn't chosen to "add extra to ordinary" that evening.

Quiet Heroes

$\mathcal{A}$ friend from my childhood recently mentioned the movie To Kill a Mockingbird. It is one of my all-time favorite stories. That got me to thinking again about my favorite type of people: Quiet Heroes.

They are the ones who are always there when needed most; the ones with a smile or a hug at just the right moment. They do the kind thing and the right thing even when the crowd is rushing the opposite way. They even put themselves In Harm's Way when that is what is needed.

So this is in honor of all the quiet heroes in my life and in the world. Thank you for making my life and my world a better place. I know there are times that it would be far more convenient and sometimes even much safer to ignore the needs of the world and I honor you for doing the kind and right thing anyway, sometimes at great risk to yourself.

I know that, like everyone else, you experience fear, exhaustion, frustration, distractions, and obstacles. And, you aren't necessarily braver than others despite accomplishing things that require extraordinary bravery and determination.

I appreciate that, like the character Atticus in the movie and book To Kill a Mockingbird you do what needs doing when it needs doing and you do it in your quiet and humble way because the cost to your soul and self-respect of not doing it would be far greater than whatever the potential cost in doing it is.

I'm grateful for that wonderful and extraordinary difference in you.

Hope for the Human Race from an Unlikely Place

A while back I saw an amazing video of a dog who ran out onto a busy highway to attempt to pull from danger another dog that had just been hit by a car. As cars whizzed by barely missing them, the heroic dog managed to get hold of the hurt canine and gradually, inch by inch, drag it to relative safety across multiple lanes of traffic to the center divide. Humans then were able to lift the wounded dog off the highway and out of harm's way. If I recall correctly, the heroic dog left the scene after it was sure the hurt one was being taken care of. I was glad to read that the wounded animal survived the ordeal and its injuries.

When I see and read stories of animals doing extraordinary things to help fellow creatures—and often creatures that are completely different species than their own—I become even more hopeful that human beings can rise above mere skin color, the shape of one's eyes, political divisiveness, and so many other things that we've allowed as justification to tear apart our brothers and sisters not just in war, but via neglect, humiliation, deprivation, cruelty, ignorance, apathy, hatred, greed, bullying, ostracizing, enslavement, and tyranny.

We have much to learn from each other and from other creatures. I firmly believe that we're interconnected and, when we do harm to another, we also do harm to ourselves and to the whole.

The Strength to Let Go

I used to hang onto painful memories or situations more out of stubbornness or habit than out of any positive reason to keep them.

Some that immediately came to mind were romantic relationship break-ups from before my marriage, a business I'd owned for 18 years and should have sold or closed years sooner than I did, and attempting to stay friends with those who had other plans or with whom I was in a toxic or detrimental relationship.

Since there were times in my life when I felt lonely and abandoned, I sometimes tended to hang on to relationships too long. I didn't want anyone to feel what I'd felt in those dark years. But in those situations, I often wasn't helping the other person and was hurting myself. In some cases I even became an enabler that inadvertently supported behavior that was hurting them because I thought I was helping.

I don't want to give up on anybody. But, sadly, there are situations where it is simply best to move on. It helps to remind myself that there are three parts to a relationship: The other person, me, and the relationship itself.

When I focus on improving the relationship and myself, rather than the other person, I often find that the relationship improves, I am becoming ever closer to the other person, and my words, actions, and vision of the best me I can be are in alignment. And I know that brings lasting happiness to me.

Unfortunately, there are times when the relationship isn't improving or is even becoming detrimental to the other person and/ or me. When that happens and when looked at from this viewpoint, it is usually simple to see that the relationship or situation should be ended.

Please note that I said "simple" rather than "easy." I've found it is often far from easy for me to end a relationship.

But I've learned that if I focus on the desire for long-term happiness of everyone in the relationship, then I'm much less likely to waste time and emotional energy blaming others or myself when a relationship ends.

And that helps me to find the strength to let go and move on.

~~~

Pain Often Led to Growth

Many of the attributes in myself that I'm most proud of (such as being strong, empathetic, and kind) are largely the direct result of the people and experiences that had "hurt" me, the feelings I had as a result, and the personal and spiritual work and growth to which all of that led me.

When that realization struck me, feelings of hurt and anger were largely and sometimes entirely replaced by appreciation and forgiveness. I found it easy to forgive when I realized the people I was forgiving had helped me to become a better person.

Being a Friend is Often One of the Most Selfish Things I Do

I rarely say aloud the words "as your friend," but I think them often. And, I almost never say or think the phrase "as my friend" about anyone or in any context.

Being a friend to others is a promise I make to myself. It is one of the most selfish things I do. I attempt to avoid making promises to others and I don't expect them to make promises to me.

My being a friend to someone really has very little to do with them. It is a gift I give to myself, as being a friend has often brought some of the greatest joys to my life.

See? I'm very selfish. Interestingly, the more selfish I am in this way, the more that I'm viewed as being a kind and loving person. SHHH! Don't tell anyone my secret! I've got a great thing going! ;-D!

I tend to be very good at sticking to promises I make to myself about others. I've learned that being a good friend, the kind of friend who attempts to be there when a friend is needed most, and who is grateful for the gift given by others when they share their grief, pain, loneliness, desperation, anguish, sadness, fear, and shame, no matter the time of day or night whenever they need someone to help or merely to listen—in other words attempting to be a friend without limits and without expectations, has brought many wonderful things to my life.

People will do or be what they are going to do or be. I attempt to focus on my actions and attitudes and have learned that when I do that my world becomes immeasurably better, and many of my relationships deeper and richer.

I hope my actions inspire the trust, faith, courage, and confidence in others to call in times of need, because it is at those times I often feel most alive, useful, worthy, trusted, and connected to that person and the universe.

~~~

Great Changes

*M*ost people have probably heard the famous quote from Mother Teresa that "Small things done with great love will change the world."

I like that saying but believe it leaves out a key point: Small things done with great love will not only change the world, they will change the person doing them in great ways, too.

And that's no small thing! ;-D!

Thank Goodness for My Failures

I think a life that never involved failing would rapidly prove dull and lifeless. If I never failed, I don't think success would be nearly as sweet.

What kind of growth would I have going forward when so far in my life many of my life's most important lessons came from learning from those times when I tried and failed? It is the not-knowing whether I'll succeed or fail at an endeavor that often adds spice to my life.

And what fun would it be to always win games, to never risk anything, to never have the opportunity to learn to fall down again and again but always get up one more time than I fell?

I think there is a great risk that, if I never failed, I'd be arrogant and intolerant of those who did. Where would my inner strength come from if I was never tested by adversity? Where would I get empathy and so many important attributes that I value in myself and humankind?

So, while I value and appreciate my successes, and in weak moments may even curse some of my failures, I know deep down inside that my failures have been even more valuable and formative to the person I've become than my successes.

Speak Softly and Carry a Big Heart

A friend who passed away several years ago was about 30 years older than me and lived large right up until his passing. He loved to surf and did so decades beyond when most people stop doing such strenuous activities. He looked more like a retired business-person than a surfer.

Mel was soft spoken and a real gentleman. He had a mustache and an impish grin. For many years after his retirement he tutored students to help them become successful in subjects in which they were struggling. He could be tough but tempered it with love.

He had a saying that I'll never forget: "Speak softly and carry a big heart."

He not only said those words, he lived by them. They are part of a legacy of love that he left with so many people whose lives he touched. Mel, and his legacy, will be remembered long after he is gone.

I'm glad Mel was in my life. I'm a better man because he was.

The Kind Road

*O*ne of my goals as a writer is that, when creating a humorous post, I want to always take the kind road, mostly laughing at myself (I can take it), while elevating and inspiring others.

I'm also much more likely to read the work of others who appear to take the kind road and avoid acidic, cutting, mean-spirited humor.

I believe that when I cut down others, wise people see through the words—no matter how "clever"—and know that I am suffering inside. Such actions tend to bring more suffering to me.

So that's why I don't understand why people—including myself when I catch myself doing it—act in a way that creates harm, pain, and divisiveness.

My Life Sweeteners

They say that if life gives you lemons make lemonade, but it has been my experience that lemonade made only with lemons is a recipe for a very bitter brew and life—and believe me I've tried!

I've found that adding sweeteners can help a lot, both in life and in lemonade. My favorite life sweeteners include love, kindness, and gratitude. When I remember to include generous helpings of each, my life becomes like a wonderfully sweet lemonade with just enough tartness to help me enjoy the sweetness all the more.

The Day the Girls Saved Me

$\mathcal{M}$any years ago I was in a high school Marine Corps JROTC program as the Vietnam War was coming to an end. It was not a real popular time to be in uniform.

It was a turbulent era. One of the many changes was that girls had been allowed to participate in the JROTC program for the first time. It was a big deal. Television crews came to the school and the female cadets ended up on TV and in the newspaper. They got so much attention that many of the male cadets were understandably jealous.

I stood up for the girls and the girls' program. Probably because I supported them, I was asked to be a sort of student teacher in the all-girls JROTC class. There was also, of course, an adult retired Marine instructor. I was there to assist him in teaching the girls. I felt honored to be trusted in this way.

I loved those girls. They were like family to me. I knew what it was like for them to wear a military uniform during the Vietnam era.

Worse for them, the girls' uniforms appeared to have been intentionally designed to make the wearer look as unattractive as possible. Their uniforms were downright ugly! And, the girls initially had to deal with the resentment of many of the male cadets.

For some reason, uniform day was on a different day that week for the girls than for the boys. On this day, the girls were in uniform. I was in civilian clothes walking about twenty feet behind them as one of the girls led them in formation down the long tunnel-like hall that ran through the center of the school.

As they marched along, three boys who were standing in a group near some lockers began taunting and jeering the girls, calling them all sorts of names.

This type of thing was something the girls had to endure a lot. I don't know what set me off that particular day. I guess that I'd just had enough.

Irritation had become anger, which had unexpectedly turned to rage.

What happened next must have been due to a brief outburst of temporary insanity. I ran toward the boys with both of my arms extended out from my sides and slammed all three of them into the lockers. The crashing sound startled everyone within 150 feet, those boys and I most of all.

I saw the looks of surprise, shock, and fear in the eyes of those boys.

Unfortunately, about two seconds later, anger was clearly their primary emotion, and my eyes must have been the ones reflecting shock, surprise, and fear as we all realized what had just happened.

They and I quickly did the math as we all came to our senses: there were three of them and only one of me. All four of us knew what was going to happen next and only three of us were going to enjoy it.

In the meantime, the girls who had been marching had heard the crashing of the boys against the lockers. They stopped and turned to see what the commotion was about and quickly realized what had just happened and just how much trouble I was in.

Two of the biggest, most athletic girls peeled from the girls' formation and stood behind and slightly to each side of me. There was no doubt in anyone's minds that the fight was no longer going to be 3 against 1.

The boys quickly re-did the math. They realized they were now in a no-win situation. Even if they won the fight, everyone in the school would know that they got into a fight with girls. And, there was always the possibility that they wouldn't win. By now, I was the least of their worries; I doubt whether I was even in their equation anymore.

I don't recall exactly what happened next. I like to think that I asked the boys to apologize to the young ladies for their insults and they did.

But it may be that the girls demanded an apology and got one or the boys apologized on their own.

I do know what didn't happen. I didn't get pounded into the ground!

I will never forget those girls. As I said, we were like family; a family that stuck together and stood up for one another. It didn't go unnoticed.

Word spread around the school about the girls standing up to the bullies and the girls were accepted and respected more after that.

He Melted Like a Candle in a Raging Furnace

I was bullied as a kid. I think most kids were. I was a short, scrawny loner, who lacked confidence in myself—in other words the PERFECT target for bullies.

Strangely, I often stood up for other kids who were being bullied, but didn't often stand up for myself when I was the target. Guess who then became the target when I stood up for those other kids?

One such incident took place in high school. It was when the Vietnam War was winding down, and the military and everyone associated with it was the butt of much anger and scorn. A buddy and I were in our Jr. ROTC U.S. Marine Corps uniforms, and a bully decided it would be great fun to rip the hat (we called them "covers") off my buddy's head and taunt him with it.

Without thinking (which tended to be my normal mode when someone else was being bullied), I rushed to my buddy's aid and stood between the bully and him. I looked up at the bully who not only was taller but bigger and stronger than me.

By now a crowd had gathered to watch the show.

Me: "Please give his cover back to him.

Bully: "Who's going to make me?"

It was about then that I realized I was once again in deep doo-doo. (I am a very slow learner and have to receive some lessons over and over again.)

Fortunately, at that moment, I noticed something that changed everything.

Sergeant Major Steele, a tall, square-jawed, muscular retired Marine and Jr. ROTC instructor saw what was happening and began walking toward us. As luck would have it, the bully was facing away from him.

I seized the moment. You've heard of liquid courage? I know something even better: Marine Corps courage.

I knew help was on the way, so I said to the bully, "You wouldn't talk that way to our Sergeant Major Steele!" I said it loudly enough that the Marine would hear it.

The bully took the bait. "Oh yes I would, I'd…"

That's as far as he got. A huge hand tapped him on the shoulder. The bully turned around to look into the eyes of a most unhappy and very large Marine glaring down at him.

"You would what, son?"

The bully melted like a candle in a raging furnace. "I, uh, I…" he stammered. "I'm sorry, sir. Then he gave my buddy's cover to me.

And that was the last time my buddy and I—or any other cadet in the whole school was ever bullied by that kid or his pals again.

Two More Bullying Stories

When I was fifteen I used to walk or ride my bicycle to work at a large buffet restaurant.

On a day I'd chosen to walk, as I neared the back door of the restaurant, a bully started taunting me and yelled that he was going to run me over with his bicycle.

I froze as he raced toward me.

A moment before he would have hit me, I took a step sideways and briefly grabbed his handle bar. What happened next surprised and scared both of us, but I'm quite sure him more than me.

I'd only meant to scare him and make his bike wobble a bit so he'd leave me alone, but neither he nor I had considered the large and thick pool of congealed grease that had leaked out of a nearby garbage bin and was immediately under us.

He flew straight over his handle bars and skidded, slid, bounced, and rolled in one direction as his bike did the same in another.

I waited until he got up so I was sure he hadn't broken anything, and then walked into the restaurant.

I never saw that kid again.

—

When I was in junior high school (also known as middle school) I was in a class with a bully who mercilessly picked on me.

I wasn't afraid of him. He was one of the few kids in school who was even smaller than me.

What I was afraid of, however, was the gang of kids that he hung out with. I was certain that, if I ever got into a fight with him, the whole gang would jump me. And as the Ron White joke goes, I wasn't sure how many of them it would take to whoop me, but I knew how many of them there were, and that's mighty handy information to have.

So day after day, week after week, I took his verbal abuse, until I finally couldn't take it anymore. I told our teacher and she said there was nothing she could do about it (which of course meant that there was nothing she WOULD do about it).

I was ashamed to tell my father, but eventually broke down and told him. He gave me the advice I'd been dreading:

"Bullies will keep picking on you until you stand up to them. They don't want to be hurt so they only pick on kids who they think won't fight back. Next time he picks a fight with you, accept the challenge. Then be sure to get in at least one good punch. Even if you lose the fight, he'll probably never pick on you again."

Oh, great. But I was so desperate for the bullying to end I decided to take his advice.

I tossed and turned for much of that night with very ugly visions of violence and pain dancing in my head.

Sure enough, the next day in class the bully came up to me and said, "I call you out!" (For those unfamiliar with the term, it means I want to fight you although I suspect you could figure that out regardless of whatever term was used where you grew up.)

I looked him in the eyes and said, "OK." I could tell I'd surprised him with that response but he quickly recovered and said, "OK!" He then demanded that I meet him behind one of the school buildings about one half hour after school ended. "And you BETTER be there!" he added with a raised fist and threatening tone.

That was the longest school day of my life. I would have done almost anything to have time stop, but to my dismay the clock betrayed me. When the last school bell of the day rang, I knew I was 30 minutes away from a terrible beating.

I figured he wanted to have the half hour after school to gather up his buddies so they could all pounce on me.

Back then, I had no friends I could count on to back me up, so it would be just me against his gang.

I knew this was the moment of truth. If I backed down now, I'd be backing down for the rest of my life. But I also was terrified of getting a broken nose and having some teeth knocked out.

I know what that Gary Cooper marshal character in the movie High Noon felt when he walked out onto the street as the clock struck 12.

It was now time for my showdown. I kept muttering as I walked to the place of my destruction, "Please, oh please, let me land just one solid punch."

I got to the appointed place, looked at my watch and was right on time. No bully.

My mind raced. At first I cheered inwardly, then thought maybe he and his gang were just running a little late. I was tempted to leave but knew that if he and his buddies showed up a few minutes later, my problem would be even worse the next day for "chickening out."

So I stayed. And waited. Then waited some more. I began to wonder how long I should wait, and decided that thirty minutes would be long enough.

A half hour after I'd arrived, I walked away, feeling proud of myself and greatly relieved.

The next day in class, before I could ask him where he'd been, he walked up to me and started talking to me as though we were best friends. But he couldn't look me in the eyes.

I never mentioned his absence, and not surprisingly neither did he. Nor did I ever find out why he didn't show up, but I suspect that was the day that he found out those thugs he thought were his "friends" weren't.

All I know for sure is that he never picked on me again and treated me with respect.

Thanks, Dad!

Bullies

I used to be so angry at bullies and ashamed of myself for, too often, not standing up to them when they came after me.

I've grown to feel sorry for bullies. I believe that no matter how much they dislike others, most probably dislike themselves even more.

It must be horrible stumbling around in the dark when there is so much beauty, light, joy, and kindness all around them.

I believe that, within nearly all people, a beautiful spirit aches to bring love and warmth into their world and ours, but it often is buried in layers of ignorance, self-loathing, critical and cynical judgments, selfishness, and similar dark debris.

May kindness be shown to these bullies, and may it begin to enlighten them—literally bring light to their world as well as to lighten their load of debris that weighs on and hides their spirit.

Darkness never drives away darkness. It takes light to do that. May they see the light and may it guide them to lasting joy and inner peace.

More on Bullying

Bullies can only keep bullying when the crowd allows, enables, or encourages it. That is true on school grounds and it is true with nations.

The cost of bullying to the bullies has got to be much greater than the reward they get for doing so.

At the global level the risk of being accused of committing crimes against humanity appear to me to be starting to have a tangible positive effect on decisions being made by at least some of the people who are inclined to slaughter people. I believe that, at least in some cases, massacres have been avoided as a result.

Humanity has a long way to go before we become truly humane but I see progress being made.

~~~

I've learned that when a man of few words speaks, it is usually wise to listen very carefully to, and learn from, those words.

The Cycle of Suffering

Some time ago I read something that I would have, at one time, agreed with and found humorous, but now just saddens me: "KARMA: No need for revenge. Just sit back and wait. Those who hurt you will eventually screw up themselves and, if you're lucky, God and/or Goddess will let you watch."

I believe that those who hurt me or others are already suffering.

May their suffering soon end, and may I be an instrument to that end.

May I forgive them for their sake and mine.

May I hope that they be enlightened rather than punished.

I believe that, until their suffering ends, it is unlikely they will stop hurting themselves and others.

May I be wise and loving enough to do my part to help end the cycle of suffering.

Re-Writing the Story

I long held onto the belief that my "biological father abandoned me when I was about four years old." Over time, I've come to realize that all I really knew is that he left when I was four years old. His leaving very likely had very little or nothing to do with me or with my siblings. I was able to release quite a lot of the emotional charge from the situation when I decided to look at it differently.

I even began to realize that my siblings and I may have made it MORE difficult for my biological father to leave instead of being a big part of the reason why he left. I simply didn't know, so it made no sense for me to make things up—especially things that had caused me so much pain: beliefs and feelings that led to abandonment issues and trying to impress people so that I'd be respected and maybe even liked (which only tended to repel them as they saw through the reasons why I was trying so hard).

The heavy weights of judgment, shame, and guilt were lifted from me when I began to open my mind to other possibilities about what really happened when I was about four years old.

I realized I'd been focusing on all the negatives from that experience. But that was only half the story. Many positives also came from what happened all those years ago: my focus on family, friends, and other important relationships is in large part due to the loneliness I'd felt as a child; perhaps, also, my empathy for others and focus on easing the pain, loneliness, and suffering of others. Much of what I've accomplished might not have occurred without that extra drive to succeed.

In other words, I began to realize that I would not be the man I am today if I hadn't experienced what I did as a young child.

I'm not suggesting that what I went through was fun or that I'd like to see anyone experience losing a parent at a young age or any other major trauma—in fact I hope for the opposite for everyone. But traumas do occur, and I've learned that, like every other aspect in life, I can choose to focus on the positives or negatives.

My life has become so much better when I've chosen to focus on the positives and be grateful for them.

So, while I believe we all have the power to make a new ending, I also believe we have the power to re-write the story of our beginning by looking at it in new ways.

To the "Rekindlers"

Some people always seem to have a ready smile, a kind word, a helping hand, a reassuring look. I call them "Rekindlers."

I believe it is no accident that the word "kind" is a big part of the word "Rekindle."

To all Rekindlers everywhere: Thank you.

A special thank you to those who rekindled my flame when it began to flicker out.

The Power of Uniters

I believe the Hunger Games stories showcase the best and worst of humankind. The power of hope, of trust, of love. The despair of poverty, hopelessness, starvation. The silliness of vanity. The rage of injustice simmering just below the thin veneer of civilization. The power of speaking simple truths in simple but honest ways. Of not letting others dictate how you will be; who you'll be. Of never giving up no matter how hopeless the odds seem to be. Of friendship and how others—including total strangers—can provide help just at the right moment in exactly the right way. The power of a hug and reassuring smile or comment. The fear dictators have of the people. The misery of slavery. The power of loyalty to those worthy of our fealty. The ways that people in power purposely divide people and pit them against each other to keep them weak and pliable. The power a uniter can have against the dividers. How one person can stand up to mighty powers and make a huge difference in the world. How a simple kindness can save a life, heal a wound, and create ripples of change for all humankind.

With Love

I often sign off from my blog posts with the words "With Love" followed by my name. That it is because I believe that anything I think, do, write, feel, or say, that doesn't involve love is wasted.

I'm not the first to have thought such things, but I find wisdom where I can, and this is a lesson that I have taken to heart.

Each time I sign my post "With Love" it is a reminder to me and to readers as to my loving intention. Readers will be able to determine for themselves as to whether love is indeed at the heart of all my written work.

I have no desire to waste my time—the precious stuff of life—creating something that isn't built on the bedrock foundation of love.

Gratitude

I believe that whoever originally coined the word "gratitude" must have consciously or subconsciously combined the words "great" and "attitude."

I believe that one needs gratitude to have a great attitude.

Or put another way, one can't help but experience gratitude when they have a great attitude.

~~~

I prefer to focus on doing, reading, watching, and listening to things that feed my soul.

Lifting the Veils

I believe I'm at my best, and my world is greatly improved, when I'm able to remove or see through (if only temporarily) the many layers of judgment, bias, pain, fear, shame, guilt, and so much more that I readily carry around with me. I can see, feel, and experience the greatness, goodness, and kindness within others and myself.

If there is some version of a heaven—and I believe there is, even if only in our own hearts—I think it is simply where and/or when the veils are lifted from our eyes, minds, and hearts, and we can all see, feel, and experience the greatness, goodness, and kindness within others and ourselves ALL THE TIME.

I've been blessed with being able to experience the greatness, goodness, and kindness within many people and other living creatures. I'm very grateful for those precious glimpses that life provides of what is beneath and all around the veils.

Smiles

They warm my heart and spirit
Never go out of style
Like beaming ones couples show
Walking together down the aisle

Nearly all are wonderful
But some mean so much more
Those from a loving family
When you walk in the door.

Some from favorite memories
The first on a baby's face
Those shared by parents
When they feel a child's embrace.

Proud but sometimes sad ones
When children have all grown
Packed up and moved out
To build lives of their own.

The kind a surgeon wears
After a long and hard fight
That says they'll pull through
Everything will be alright.

They are so often present
When I travel down
Memory Lane
Think back to favorite scenes
To experience them again.

Choices

*W*henever I receive an email or other message with a link and a note that says something to the effect that opening it is a fun way to waste time, I immediately delete the message without opening the link.

It just happened again, but as I deleted the message, I paused for a moment to ask myself why I have such a reaction to these types of messages.

The answer immediately came to me:

I don't see them as a waste of time, but as a waste of precious life. I know that when I'm on my death bed I won't regret my decision. I'll be grateful for having used such moments to connect with people and to experience all the beauty and miracles that life has to offer instead. Life is too short and too precious for me to consider doing anything less.

After all, today—this moment—could (and someday will) be my last in this life, it would be a tragedy for me to waste it.

Beyond My Blindness

When I focus on things that help me grow
I find all kinds of time to get back in the flow

When I focus on things that make me laugh
That's when I know I'm on the right path

When I focus on things that make me feel
I find whole new ways to help me heal.

When I focus on things like love and kindness
I begin to see beyond my blindness

If I Could Only Give One Message to the World

We all have the power to create our own heaven and hell right here on Earth.

We can focus on becoming more kind, compassionate, generous, forgiving, and loving, and, by doing so, become surrounded by kind, compassionate, generous, forgiving, and loving people, or we can take the opposite approach and be surrounded by unkind, uncaring, greedy, unforgiving, and hateful people.

The choice is ours, every waking moment of every day of our lives.

~~~

Adversity and Me

I can choose to let adversity
Weaken or strengthen me
The choice is mine
Every time

Terrible Times, and Choices

Some of the kindest, most giving, and empathic people I know have experienced some pretty awful things in their lives. Then again, some people who do some terrible things also appear to have experienced many terrible things in their own lives. To a large extent, I believe it is a choice—like so many other choices we have each day, but one that often comes with much larger consequences.

Some will use their experiences as a way to help others, and some will use them as an excuse to hurt them. But, many who head down the latter path can change their choices with the faith, love, hope, coaching, and kindness of others, often especially from those who have walked such paths before them and know where they lead unless a different way is chosen in time.

~~~

I've found that, most often, fighting against something creates more violence and destruction, while loving towards something often creates healing of the human spirit and our world.

No Need for a Key

Searched for the key to happiness
Sought joy from far and wide
Looked everywhere I could think of
But never looked inside
Then one day it came to me
When I stopped to take a rest

How much time I wasted
In my search for happiness
Knew then that I'd been wrong
In that which I had supposed
For all the time I'd sought the key
The door had never been closed!

The Great Blindini

I have a friend named Brent. He's blind. He is also a magician. He calls himself The Great Blindini.

He has a great perspective on life that includes an excellent fun sense of humor.

Instead of telling his audiences "Now you see it, now you don't," he says "Now you see it, now I don't."

When my children were young, he used to entertain them with his magic.

Brent considers himself a teacher. He tries to help others and be an example for them.

He's had to overcome a lot of fear to do that. He says that everything you do comes down to love or fear.

It doesn't take long being around Brent before it's clear that he is doing what he loves.

An Unexpected Pleasure

I may have mentioned a time or two that it sometimes takes a while for me to become human in the morning—and often involves substantial amounts of caffeine in order to do so. This is about one of those mornings.

I was jarred awake by the ringing of both my alarm clock and my business phone. I jumped out of bed and, while trying to clear my head of morning fog, tried to figure out which annoying sound to deal with first. I ended up leaning forward with my arms out of position and did a slow-motion low-speed crash into the wall with my forehead as the impact point.

I no doubt muttered something to myself. I have no clue what it was but it probably wasn't fit to hear anyway.

Shaking loose the cobwebs in my head, I stumbled as fast as I could to my work phone two rooms away and got to it between the 4th and 5th ring, picking up the receiver just as the caller hung up … and left no message.

(In case you're wondering whether all of that was the "unexpected pleasure" part of the post as advertised in the title, rest assured that it was not. While it might seem that sometimes I'm a glutton for punishment, I am more of a glutton for pleasure kind of guy.)

Then the dogs wanted to go outside. Then inside. Then outside. I finally got back to my desk, precious coffee in hand, when a dog barked outside my window. I work best without a lot of distractions and with a lot of quiet, so let's just say that, up to that point, I wasn't the happiest or most productive person you'll ever meet.

That dog's bark was one irritation too many. That was it, I was DONE! I turned in my chair to look through the window on my right and filled my lungs in preparation for a very loud yell when, mid-breath, my eyes caught a rose bush just outside my window that had exploded into a glorious display of floral beauty with perfect white flowers and buds that were illuminated by a sun that had just burned through what had been an overcast sky.

It was a view of perfection less than three feet from where I sat that I'd been too blind to see.

I never got the yell out. The dog stopped barking on its own. What began as just another negative in a growing list of them this morning became a wonderful reminder as to the beauty, wonders, blessings, and joy all around me when I open my eyes, mind, and attitude, to experience them.

That set the tone for another glorious day.

Morning Reflections

*T*here was a time many years ago when I woke up exhausted every week day, crawled out of bed at about 5:30 a.m. and faced a daunting and life-sucking 1 hour and 40 minute one-way commute to work, doing a job I came to dislike, and then to dread. It was hard on My Beloved and me. She was left alone in a strange town with two young children, and her friends and family were two hours away. It was a low point in our lives and marriage.

As I drove to work, I felt trapped and stupid for ever having gotten myself and my family into the situation. Every penny we could scrape together had been sunk into the relocation and new home, the house wasn't appreciating, closing costs at both ends meant we'd lose everything if we quickly sold the house, and the closest job I could get was an insanely long distance away. We endured it for two long, long years.

Fast-forward about 32 years. My typical morning starts with a kiss from My Beloved (always a good way to start my day). Our dogs come over to snuggle me and get their first scratch of the day. I get some coffee and begin my commute. It takes all of about 15 seconds to get to my office. I "work" from home. I put quotes around that word because what I do professionally feels a lot more like play and pleasure than what most people would consider "work." It even started as a hobby; then friends and family asked me to do it for them; then they convinced me that I should do it professionally, so I now I get paid to do what I love: managing investment portfolios for clients.

A window in my office is open and I hear the birds singing. I look out to see my small redwood grove and fern garden in all its glory as the sun filters through and the wind plays to a beat only it knows, creating a slow-moving kaleidoscope of many shades of green with reddish-brown accents.

I sip my coffee and turn on my computer. My constant companion, a chocolate lab named Duke, is nestled at my feet. My "work" day has begun.

It took too long for me to figure out that I had much more control of my own destiny than I'd dared to imagine—as I said, I'm a slow learner. It also took a lot of effort, some risk, and the courage to dream and to take action every day toward turning my dreams into reality, but with the encouragement and support of friends and family my dreams have come true.

You see, although I'm a slow learner, I often do eventually "get" the lessons that life so patiently tries to teach.

As I reflect back on less happy times, such as that grueling commute and life of so many years ago, I'm reminded once again of how blessed I am. And immensely grateful.

Dreams and What Actually Happens

I used to say to people "May your dreams come true." I've learned, quite frequently, that isn't what leads a person to lasting joy.

I'm now more likely to say, "May your dreams come true, or may what actually happens be far greater than you ever dreamed possible."

~~~

Where the Magic Is

*Y*our heart is where the magic is. When your heart connects with the hearts of others, amazing and wonderfully touching, inspiring, and sometimes even transformational things can occur.

Life Is a Magnifier

I believe that life is a magnifier and will magnify good and ill deeds out into the world and back onto the doer. I'm not suggesting that life is always fair—I've seen too many examples where it isn't—but I still believe in karma and that good deeds tend to create a better world, and bad deeds tend to have the opposite effect, so it makes sense to me to choose kindness, compassion, love, empathy, and gratitude over actions that harm or ignore the needs of others.

~~~

Gratitude can turn a negative into a positive. Find a way to be thankful for your troubles and they can become your blessings.

My Recipe for Life

I believe most people feel that life is very complex and complicated. That is understandable. There is so much information, regulation, conflicting needs and priorities, entities telling and selling what we need and should do, partisanship and rancor, choices, stresses, demands on our time, attention and loyalties, and conflicting deadlines that humankind has to deal with every day that it makes it very easy to become completely overwhelmed.

I've found that, by identifying the relatively few things that are most important—that truly matter—to me, and investing nearly all of my time, energy, attention, love, and passion on them, that most of those far less important distractions gradually fade away.

And, as they do, I've found much greater contentment, happiness, fulfillment, confidence, and inner peace.

I'm incredibly fortunate to be able to spend nearly all day every day doing what I truly love to do. They include investing time with family and friends, having a very flexible schedule so that I'm nearly always available when loved ones need or want to be with me, and doing what I love and what inspires me both professionally and with my hobbies.

That doesn't mean I have life by the tail or that I or my life are perfect. Far from it. I'm a slow learner in the school of life and have many more mistakes to make and lessons to learn.

I'm incredibly blessed to be surrounded by people who patiently tolerate my many imperfections and love me in spite of—or sometimes perhaps even because of—them. They coach, guide, comfort, cajole, teach, and support me. But most important of all, they love me.

~~~

Enriching My Life with Love

Life is short and getting shorter, so I'm focused on making more of my remaining time richer by investing what I do with love.

With practice I'm getting better at it but I've still got a long way to go before I'm able to enrich every remaining thought, word, and action of my life with love.

I may in fact never get there but I know that my life will be immeasurably improved by this focus—and hopefully the lives of others as well.

A Grandsons' List is a Bucket List
with More Magic Poured In

$\mathcal{A}$ walk in nature with our senses fully open and aware can be a truly spiritual and awe-inspiring reawakening. Even better would be to do so with a young child for which everything is new and magical. I look forward to walking with my grandsons in a redwood grove, along a forest trail near a stream, on the beach near the ocean, camping under the stars, and so many more magical places.

In the meantime, I'll patiently wait for them to reach an age where we can do those things together and keep adding to my Grandsons' List. (It's like a Bucket List with magic poured in!) ;-D!

The Eyes of a Child

*M*any people say they feel old when they become a grandparent, but I'm feeling young again. Between my three children and my three grandsons, this will be the sixth time that I'll get to experience and explore life through the eyes of a child—and that NEVER gets old to me.

Every bug, rock, leaf, raindrop, and rainbow take on a whole new sense of wonder, awe, and amazement, and are worthy of much time and contemplation. Puddles become playgrounds. "Walks" become stops, to take the time to REALLY LOOK at the wonders and miracles all around us. In the meantime, just gazing into the eyes of my infant and toddling grandchildren as they gaze into mine, is more than enough for me.

~~~

The Dance

Dappled shadows on our path
Filtered light through verdant leaves
Treading softly hear the whispers
Ancient dance of wind and trees.

"Cheerfulness and contentment are great beautifiers
and are famous preservers of youthful looks."

—Charles Dickens (Source: Wordsmith.org)

Dickens' comment inspired me to write this poem:

Beautifiers

I agree
They are indeed
And believe
Those attributes
And attitudes
Along with kindness
And gratitude
Beautify lives
And worlds.

It's the Little Things

*O*ne summer afternoon I was using a garden hose to hand-water a rose bush. It was thirsty, so I stood in one place as the stream showered its liquid life on the plant. To my right, about four feet away is about a ten-foot tall plant covered in beautiful purple flowers.

As I silently stood admiring it, out of the corner of my eye a little feathery flash flew into the tall bush.

I stood motionless to see if the tiny bird might show itself again.

To my delight and surprise, first one, then two, and soon a total of six little feathered friends showed themselves as they danced from branch to branch as if to a merry tune that only they could hear.

One even jumped onto one of the top branches of the rose bush I was watering. I made sure that the spray never quite reached the bird but put the stream close enough so a little mist could cool the tiny creature. It was clear he was enjoying himself immensely.

He even scratched his cheek by rubbing it on a stem.

I knew the magic would end as soon as I moved to water the next rose bush, so I lingered a bit, soaking up the moment and making a memory.

Then I moved, and in a flash they were gone.

Rainstorm and Rainbow Revelry
on a Cloudless Day

I love rain drops and rainstorms, reveling in the many sounds they make, the feel of raindrops on my skin, the sight of each drop as it splash-dances onto whatever it touches, the way they freshen the air, and the gift of life bestowed by their very presence.

Sunny days are the norm where I live in California. Rainy days are often few and far between. So, I often water my small redwood grove and fern garden. I do it by hand with a watering hose and it is truly a labor of love.

Today as I watered, I noticed the sound of the water hitting some ancient plants—their predecessors date back to the age of the dinosaurs—and closed my eyes to focus on the musical way the sounds changed as the spray shifted onto various parts of the long, slender plants, much as wind and chimes make their own melody as a gift for all who take the time to experience and appreciate.

I kept my eyes closed, soaking in the rainy melody, feeling the refreshing mist on my sun-warmed body, grateful for the moment, making the moment last, and creating another beautiful memory.

My eyes stayed shut as I sprayed other plants, changing the melody that nature so generously provided to me.

I imagined myself in a wondrous rainstorm while out in nature, and felt at home in its welcoming arms.

I felt warm, safe, fully alive and present, serenity, and an inner peace in that embrace.

Feelings of joy and gratitude swept over me.

I was hesitant to break the spell, but there were other things that needed to be done, so I knew I would soon need to open my eyes and move on with my day.

But before I did, I adjusted the spray nozzle once more.

When I opened my eyes, a glorious rainbow appeared. I knew it would be there; a beloved friend who appears when water and sun come together in just the right ways to co-create yet another stunning and truly inspiring miracle.

Earth's Music

From the rhythm of ocean waves
To the dance by sun and moon
Everything has a cadence
If we listen for its tune.

Enchanted

Some folks say
there's too much silence
When they're out in the country
If only they could hear
All the sounds that inspire me
Sunrise brings out the birds
As they begin their own songs
Except the Mockingbird
who knows them all
And simply sings along
Each drop of rain from the storm
Makes a melody
And the voices of a waterfall
Sing in harmony
The leaves on each tree
Sway to every tune
When darkness falls
the coyotes howl
Their love song to the moon
They all come together
in a wondrous way
To sing and play for me

I'm enchanted by the forest choir
And nature's symphony
With every note of music
Each whisper of the wind
When I'm away from the country
I can't wait to get back again
Because nature comes together
in a wondrous way
To sing and play for me
I'm enchanted by the forest choir
And nature's symphony

Amma's Surprise

Several years ago I accepted a friend's invitation to see Mata Amritanandamayi who is far more commonly known as simply "Amma" (which if I recall correctly means "Mother" in her culture). I apologize to readers of that culture for my ignorance. I certainly mean no disrespect to you or to Amma.)

Many thousands come to visit and be hugged by Amma, so she is sometimes referred to as the "Hugging Saint."

At the time of the invitation I knew nothing about her, but I trusted my friend and figured it would be an interesting adventure.

When we arrived, I was surprised by the huge crowd that had come to be hugged (and blessed?) by her. The longer I stayed among them the more I noticed how much love and kindness the crowd exuded. It was palpable.

I was impressed that so many kind and loving people would come to see her—tens of thousands each visit.

I became more intrigued by the whole experience. There was such a huge crowd that numbers or pieces of paper with times on them—I don't remember which—were given to each new person arriving. That way only a small subset of the people would have to wait in line at one time. Either way, although we'd come fairly early, it quickly became clear that the hugging was going to go on all night and that our turn would be sometime in the wee morning hours. It was a week night and we both had to work the next day.

My friend said that was not a problem with this crowd of people and he was right. When he mentioned our situation, two people with much earlier numbers or times stepped forward and volunteered to swap with ours.

Their kindness and generosity was wonderful to experience!

What was a bit less wonderful was that the two people weren't from the same group and that meant my friend and I would each see Amma separately, but it was no big deal because there were lots of things to do, foods to try, and interesting shops to check out while the other was in line.

My friend's time/number came up first so he was hugged by Amma. Then it was my turn to get into the long line as my friend went exploring all the wonderfully rich sights, sounds, and aromas.

Gradually the line ahead of me got shorter, and then it was my turn. I approached her. She looked like a kind woman who was in her 50's. Her hug was indeed loving and quite pleasant. I don't recall exactly what accompanied her hug, but I believe she whispered something in her language into an ear of each person as she hugged them. Perhaps a volunteer translated what she said to the person being hugged, but I don't recall. She may also have handed something (a token or a flower?) to each person as she hugged them. (I sure wish my memory was better!)

But it was what happened next that I will never forget. As our hug was complete and I began to move away from her to let the next person in line have their hug, Amma turned to a volunteer and said something to them in her language. The volunteer called to me and said that Amma had requested that I remain on the stage with her.

Her request caught me completely by surprise. I could tell that I was being honored by the request but had no idea as to why. I'd seen many people who had been in line ahead of me get their hug and go.

Why me? Why was I being asked to stay? I hadn't spoken a word to Amma. Our eyes had met only briefly, and the hug probably only lasted 10-30 seconds (again, I don't recall). I didn't speak her language, was not from her culture, or her belief or tradition. (I heard later that, when someone had asked her what her religion was, she replied her religion was love.)

I wanted to honor her request and thought it would be rude to leave, and I have to admit I felt honored by her request, so I stayed on the crowded stage as she continued hugging the never-ending line of people.

Time passed. I sat with the question, but no answers came.

I suddenly remembered my friend and that at some point he'd come looking for me in the huge crowd in the large multi-building site. I knew he would know that my hug had ended quite a bit earlier and it was very unlikely that he would look on the stage to find me.

As time passed I grew increasingly concerned that my friend wouldn't be able to find me.

Ironically, at a time and place that I should have been relaxed and greatly enjoying the experience and the honor, I was getting increasingly anxious.

I was torn between possibly being disrespectful to Amma—a

person who clearly was greatly respected by everyone there and who had honored me with her kind request—and letting my friend know where I was.

I kept looking for him in the crowd to motion to him and get his attention, but I never saw him.

The tension built inside me. I don't recall if I eventually signaled to a volunteer that I had to leave or they could tell by my body language and pained expression that I needed to go and signaled it was OK. Either way, while I was sad to go, I was also greatly relieved to be able to find my friend.

I found him, explained what had happened, and we headed home.

I'm grateful for the gift Amma gave me by asking me to stay, and I still sometimes wonder why Amma chose me from among so many others she hugged. I don't know if I was the only one chosen—I greatly doubt it—but I also doubt that it was random chance and I don't recall seeing her choose anyone else during the fairly long time I was on the stage with her either.

I guess I'll never know. And perhaps that is yet another gift she gave to me that night.

Thank you for the wonderful and mysterious surprise, Amma!

Each Day

At this stage in life there's no doubt
I've far less future and far more past
But at least I've figured out
Make each day count and make it last

~~~

May my heart enhance my vision, and spirit shine through my eyes and actions.

"If Only ..."

"If only…" he said
'til the day he died
Let regrets drown
His dreams inside

Paralyzed in the present
By mistakes of the past
Gave up on living
Until dying at last

Few words are so cruel
Or have ruined more lives
They corrode the spirit
And cut like knives

Two little words
But oh the cost
Dreams shattered
And lives lost

Don't suffer the fate
Of broken-winged birds
Time to break free
From those two little words

The Toughest Nuts to Crack

*I*t has been my experience dealing with hundreds of men in various trainings over the years that the toughest nuts to crack often have some of the biggest hearts.

They develop a fierce persona to protect themselves from further pain.

When they "go fierce" and are met by fierce love, magic often occurs—a thing so beautiful that my eyes fill up just thinking about it.

A buddy actually goes into the hardest-core prisons as an unpaid volunteer to try to help change the futures of as many of those men as he can. I honor his courage and dedication to men who society has largely written off.

Broken Promise

An unopened bud
A leaf left uncurled
A loss of great beauty
To a beckoning world
Withered by fear
From memories and pain
Won't risk rejection
Shame and disdain
Unrealized potential
Hidden deep in a ball
They suffer in silence
A broken promise to all
Kindness can open
Closed buds over time
Heal shattered hearts
And fearful minds
A bud can be opened
By the love of a friend
Who believes in their dreams
So their spirit can mend

Sometimes it takes
The smallest of sparks
A word to encourage
Those alone in the dark
Nurturing love
Can go a long way
To help beautiful petals
Feel the light of day
Bask in the glory
Of knowing they dared
Make the world better
By the beauty they shared
Often late bloomers
Are most lovely of all
As their beauty is deeper
From their time in the ball

My Biggest Fear

I fear foolishly letting minor hassles, annoyances, pet peeves, biases, and false beliefs distract me from all the beauty, love, blessings, and kindness in the world so that, instead of feeling gratitude and seizing every precious moment and opportunity of every day, I waste them.

I can't think of a greater tragedy than letting my life slip away a moment at a time without appreciating and giving something wonderful in return.

~~~

A s darkness recedes when light appears, it has been my experience that negative emotions immediately begin to recede when positive emotions appear.

In Such Awareness Gratitude Grows

I believe that most people could come up with a list of hundreds of blessings if they took the time to think about them.

Some of my greatest blessings sure didn't feel like blessings at the time they happened. For example, having my fiancée leave me for another man was devastating at the time, but about a year later My Beloved came into my life—and has made it better ever since. Had I been married to my original fiancée I'd have missed the love of my life.

I encourage people to take another, closer look at events and experiences that they've carried in their minds as some of their biggest or worst "disasters," "failures," and "heart-breaks."

I believe that when people do this they are likely to find some of their greatest blessings and gifts ultimately came from such painful experiences.

Sometimes it just takes a while and an open mind to find out what good came from them.

In such awareness, gratitude grows.

~~~

Bitterness fades away when I focus on the sweet things in life.

Jigsaw Sculpture

I am occasionally asked regarding how or where I get ideas for my poems, lyrics, and short stories. The ideas come from everywhere and everything. Sometimes a single word or phrase ignites a spark of an idea. Sometimes it is a photograph, a smell that brings up a memory, something I see in nature, a person, or an action.
To me, it is a matter of seeing the same things everyone else sees, but looking at them differently, from unusual angles, or as though with different lighting, or through a prism.

This morning, for example, I saw California poppies as I left the house. That brought up the phrase "Gold Fever" and that phrase led in several creative directions.

On any given day I often have multiple such inspirations. Sometimes I let them sit for a while to see how strong the pull is toward the idea, and other times I immediately begin writing and don't stop until I'm done.

In either case, I've found that it is important to immediately write down the idea. I've lost some wonderful ideas because I didn't have a way to capture them at the time, and then got distracted and forgot what they were. Now, I almost always have within arm's reach a way to capture ideas.

Perhaps strangely, some of my best ideas come when I am in the bathroom, mowing lawns, or doing something tedious. I believe that it may be because my brain has more bandwidth and freedom to be creative at such times.

Taking a seed of an idea and fleshing it out feels a lot like putting together a jigsaw puzzle, gradually adding pieces, creating an outline in a basic shape, trying different things to see what fits, expanding the picture, etc.

Then when the puzzle is put together, the next phase is like sculpting. The completed jigsaw puzzle is typically mostly two-dimensional, but I want my work to be 3-dimensional. At this point, I equate the project to be more akin to a block of marble.

It might be a beautiful block of marble, but I want it to be so much more. Now, rather than adding, I attempt to chip away at the block as sculptors do, to reveal something that was there all the time and was bursting to show itself.

The challenge is to remove just the right amount of the block to reveal the essence of the piece.

I know that I have succeeded when the completed work moves people. If they feel one or more emotions, that is good, but if they feel connected and/or inspired, that is great.

I feel that my writing is making a positive difference when I get feedback from readers that something I created moved them to tears—joyous or healing—or inspired them to cast off something that has not been working in their lives, or to try something new.

There are few things that make me feel more wonderful than knowing I'm making a positive difference in the world, whether it is in the life of a single person or many.

The Flow

*O*ften out of the blue I get an inspiration, idea, thought, impression, or feeling.

I've learned that, rather than fight what is coming up for me, it is best to simply embrace and record the jumbled rush of thoughts and feelings as a scribe would when his master speaks. But unlike a scribe, I don't feel subservient. I feel blessed to be given a gift; a sacred trust.

I often have to furiously write lest some critical pieces be forgotten and lost forever. When the flow starts, I sometimes have no idea what form it will eventually become; a song, story, poem, or something else entirely.

It's like being a boat on a mysterious river not knowing what I will encounter around the bend.

I've learned to trust the flow, and believe it has been entrusted to me to share it, as I believe we all are given gifts that are intended to be shared.

While our gifts may be different, I believe that each is valuable and important.

I feel an obligation to share mine. It is as though they are merely being loaned to me and the true owners are those who would be touched by the gifts that flow through me.

Facing the Mirrors

Has my
Courage
Held up
On my
Darkest days?
Have I helped
Those in need
Along the way?

When facing
Such mirrors
It's clear
To see
I've got
More work
To do
On me.

Living Life Inside Out

I used to keep nearly all of myself hidden deep inside, afraid as to how the world would react if they could see the real me. And, sometimes, when I screwed up enough courage to let a little of myself out as a youngster and even as an adult, there were often people who delighted in making fun of me or ridiculing my ideas. So, I'd go run and hide inside again. It hurt too much to have people ridicule me or my ideas, or worse to me in some ways, completely ignore or not acknowledge the changes I was making and the creations I began to share.

But over time, as I continued working on myself, I began to attract more people into my life who I could count on to celebrate the changes and creations occurring within me that I increasingly shared with the world. Readers of this book are a part of that, and I'll be forever grateful.

I am now living my life inside-out, sharing the real me, and loving life much more than I've ever done before.

With All I've Got

I began writing my first book in May 2013, and have written seven books since then (in about 6 months).

I received a comment from a reader mentioning that my whole writing experience has mushroomed in the short time she has known me. She wondered if I ever dreamed that everything would come together as fast as it did ...

Her comment was a wonderful opportunity to pause and reflect. I realized that I didn't have an immediate answer.

After some thought, this was my reply: "Your kind comments led me to think about whether I ever dreamed about such things, etc. I think writing was one of many dreams I had throughout life that I knew were highly unlikely to come true such as many people have regarding becoming a professional ball player, a superstar actor, or winning a Nobel Peace Prize.

"Once I realized that I had at least some modest ability to write song lyrics a few years ago, my pipe dreams regarding other types of writing seemed to me to feel a little less farfetched.

"As I don't tend to enjoy long projects—another reason that writing a full-length nonfiction book seemed very unlikely—I began to try short projects such as blog postings, poetry, and then children's books, and found that I also loved those forms of writing.

"Always, in the back of my mind, I thought some of my original stories and blog posts might be of interest to readers as part of a book, but since I don't enjoy long projects and do like to focus on doing things I love to do, writing a nonfiction book still seemed to be more of a pipe dream—until 2 or 3 days ago.

"What changed? I don't really know. All of a sudden I had the passion to write a nonfiction book that I'd never had before. I've learned that, once my passion for something flares, I need to go for it with all I've got as I never know how long it will be until something else comes along for which my passion burns even brighter."

I think going for something with all I've got as long as my passion burns brightly for it is the wisest way for me to live. In fact, I can't imagine living any other way.

For You

Some may like what I write
Maybe many or just a few
Regardless of the number
I'll write for those who do.

~~~

Acceptance and Inner Peace

I believe that, when one grows to love and accept even the parts of themselves they are most ashamed of or embarrassed by—as soul mates and kindred spirits often do—greater inner peace is likely.

Change

I believe I have changed far more in the last three years than during any prior seven-year period during my adult life.

People often talk of how much courage it takes to change, and that is often true.

After the fact, I've identified three major underlying fears that I had to face in order to change:

Losing those I love

Failing

Looking foolish

It was at the moment when I realized that, no matter how much or how little I chose to change, the people who truly love me will always love me, and those who don't, won't. It doesn't matter what I do or don't do. That realization was very freeing, enabling, and inspiring.

Even the risks of failing or feeling silly became much less daunting when I realized that I'd already often failed and done foolish things, and those who truly loved me stood by me and even supported me until I could regain my balance.

The fears of losing those I love, failing, and looking foolish, were a toxic brew that crippled me far too long. But, as soon as they were dispelled by the truth, change took far less courage and even became fun and relatively easy, leading to a personal creative renaissance unlike I've ever experienced.

Whispered Wisdom

*F*or much of my life I felt lonely when I was alone. Then I began working from home and being alone all day and grew to love it. It was during those hours of solitude that I began to hear much more clearly what my heart and spirit had been whispering to me all along.

~~~

*S*o much misery comes from settling for less than we can be in life and doing less than we can do.

No Doubt

I have
No doubt
That it
Is when
I look
Within
That I
Will thrive
Without

Going From Negativity to Positivity

When I want to go from negativity to positivity, I
  Smile (even when I don't feel like it).
  Watch a comedy with a happy ending to help put laughter back
      into my life.
  Read blogs of people whose posts warm my heart.
  Count my blessings.
  Spend time with people I love.
  Read an inspiring or uplifting book.
  Go out in nature and sit and take it all in.
  Stop and take time to breathe deeply and think of things that
      are going right in my life and world.
  Take a moment to think of all the miraculous things that are
      going on in my body every microsecond.
  Read inspiring quotes and affirmations.
  Call a friend.
  Perform a kindness.
  Unclutter a part of my life, such as clean off my desk.

Mirages

It happened without warning
One moment everything was clear
Then my eye glasses broke
And my life became a blur

But my fuzzy vision
Brought into sharp relief
That what happened to my eyes
Can happen to my beliefs

Opinions built on air
Come crashing to the ground
And sometimes "facts" no longer fit
With biases brought down

Now my eyes once again
See with clarity
With help from my new glasses
That are a better fit for me

But what about my false beliefs
When they're shattered on the ground?
And the mirages I had counted on
Are nowhere to be found?

The Other Side of Me

It is important to me that you see all aspects of me, not just the positive attributes.

There is another side of me that I want you to know: the small and petty side; the weak and selfish, impatient, disappointed, and angry side; the Stinking Thinking, Pity-Party, Woe-Is-Me, nothing-is-good-enough side. I, too, often have an awful case of Baditude. I think that word pretty accurately (actually, "UGLY accurately" would be closer to the truth!) describes a side of me that wants to scowl and frown in the face of incredible blessings. This side makes me not even want to be with me in those moments.

This is a side that my friends and family love me in spite of, for which I'm eternally grateful.

Readers who've never met me may never see this side if I don't share it with you, too. I'm not sure about the reasons why this is important to me, but it is.

Perhaps it is partly because I'd feel like a phony if I were liked for only the best parts of me.

While part of me says I shouldn't care what others think, the truth is that I do. I'd much rather risk having people dislike me for who I truly am than to have them like only a false vision of me.

The truth is that I'm humble, but I'm also arrogant, and sometimes even vain. I'm a hero and a coward. I have both great and petty thoughts. I sometimes think I've got life well in hand and sometimes think that I don't have a clue. I'm generous and selfish. Wise and foolish. Proud and ashamed. I write to give and to get.

This hasn't been easy for me to write, but it is perhaps one of the most important things to me to have written.

Thank you for reading it.

~~~

A Tough Teacher

When I begin to believe
I've got life licked
It shows me in many
Not-so-subtle ways
That I'm far from
Mastering it.

Three Little Words

Sometimes kind people do unkind things, and it can be a kindness to privately point out the unkindness in a kind way.

Often the three little words "That was unkind" said in a gentle and loving way can have a major positive impact on the words and actions of otherwise kind people.

~~~

My Dream

I dream of the blessed day
when humanity awakens
from its terrible nightmare
and begins to work for peace
with as much ferocity, tenacity,
and heroism as we've fought our wars.

The Tyrant

I always have to be vigilant against a dastardly tyrant that—if I let him—can suck the joy and spontaneity out of my life, and keep me cowering in the cages of fear, self-doubt, loathing, vanity, and false feelings of unworthiness. He has a name: My Ego.

~~~

Ego-Driven Thoughts

I've found that most negative, disempowering, envious, debilitating, and anger-inducing thoughts are ego driven, and once I label them as such I've found it is much easier to quickly dismiss them and move on to more positive and uplifting ones rather than dwelling on the negative and re-running a series of old and negative messages my ego tends to conjure up if I let it.

Feeding the Ugliness within Me

Some of my greatest learning has come when I looked at the reasons why someone's words or actions repelled me. When I looked inside myself I often found things that made me uncomfortable and disappointed in myself. Not a fun place to be at all! No wonder my ego so badly wanted me to turn my back in those situations.

But when I let my ego take charge of my actions and thoughts, I only fed the ugliness within myself.

When I resisted the urge to turn away, I began to experience the greatness of the spirit within others, and began to notice how much better I began to feel about myself in the process.

It hasn't been a quick or easy transformation—I'm a very slow learner and there is a whole lot of ugly to deal with—but it was an important one for me.

I also sometimes forget lessons and have to re-learn them, but that, too, is sadly a normal part of my learning process.

The Corrosive Power of Ego

I believe that ego corrodes relationships, self-confidence, and feelings of self-worth. My ego used to run nearly constant unnecessary and harmful replays in my mind of instances that happened long ago that brought on feelings of shame, guilt, pain, and embarrassment, and since I didn't know any better, I used to let my ego get away with it to terrible effect.

Over time, I've gradually learned a way that works much better for me and built it into a habit that has freed my mind to focus on things that nourish rather than poison it.

Whenever I catch myself thinking about an incident that brings on feelings of shame, guilt, pain, and embarrassment, I attempt to ask myself: "have you learned the lesson(s) and accepted the gift(s) life gave to you when those experiences occurred?"

If my answer is yes, I remind myself that my ego is replaying a scenario in my mind that is no longer needed and is harming me. Then I change the subject in my mind.

This approach has made a world of difference in my life, and I count it among the many blessings for which I'm grateful.

Poetry? Are You Nuts?

When I began to consider writing my first poem as an adult in October, 2012, I remember thinking:

"Poetry? Am I nuts? What do I know about writing poetry? What am I thinking?

"I'm not a poet!" Then I wrote a poem and became one. Then another poem, and another.

I've probably written well over 100 poems in my first year as a poet.

Some, in my judgment, stank. Others actually seemed to be pretty decent.

As a new poet, they are all part of my journey.

I found it interesting but not completely surprising that some folks seemed to really like my stinkers, and others weren't fond of the ones that I thought were decent.

That's why I decided to share them all with those expressing an interest in hearing them instead of self-censoring.

Hopefully, over time my decent-to-stinker ratio will improve.

In the meantime, I'm having fun.

I had to ignore all the self-defeating self-talk by realizing that it was only my ego trying to protect me from pain, and focus on what my heart and spirit were telling me.

I've found that my ego often lies to me, but my spirit is as true as the North Star.

The Small Picture

I sometimes get overwhelmed by the "Big Picture." When that happens, I find it helps me when I stop and take several deep breaths, and start focusing on the small picture for a while. That gives my subconscious brain a chance to keep working on a possible answer while I distract my overly-active conscious brain with a chore or with the beauty of a sunset or silhouette. Then, often when I least suspect it, my subconscious provides the answer. I just have to give it a quiet space to do so.

~~~

Surprise!

*T*o my surprise, the more of myself I shared with others—idiosyncrasies, weirdness, and all—the more I've actually liked what I've seen. It took a while to get used to it—perhaps I'm an acquired taste even to myself—but I'm often pleasantly surprised with what comes out of each experience that I have with my heart and spirit.

Every Gift Has Someone Who Will Appreciate It

*O*ne rarely accomplishes anything worthwhile by hiding in a crowd. If we aren't sticking out, then we are hiding the gifts that we could be giving to the world.

We all have something to share and some time ago I decided that I was no longer willing to keep hiding mine and who and what I am.

I used to fear rejection, but I came to realize that, for every gift (no matter what it is or who is offering them), there will be some who will appreciate it and some who won't.

Hiding or sharing my gifts won't change that.

Hiding them just says I'm ashamed of them and of myself, and fear what others will think of them.

Sharing them says I'm proud of who I am and of the gifts I have to offer to those who will enjoy them. I like this way of being and am never going back to the person who was afraid to share my gifts.

It is my hope that those of us who share our messages and gifts may be able to inspire much younger people—and all people—to find and share their gifts and to be proud of them.

I Changed My View and It Changed Me

*T*here were times many years ago when I thought my friends had abandoned me. I was wrong. I had only thought that they and I were friends. I hadn't really been much of a friend to them so I shouldn't have been surprised when they weren't there for me either. I learned that, to have better friends, I needed to consistently BE a much better friend. Now I have true friends because I became one.

I also learned that sometimes people who I didn't consider to be friends came through for me anyway. I'd been selling them short and not appreciating them as much as I should.

I decided that much like the saying there are two kinds of people, those who believe that nothing is a miracle and those who believe that everything is, I'd begin to believe and live my life based on the premise that nearly everyone is a friend or potential friend. My life has been far richer since I changed my view and it changed me.

A Powerful Motivator

A reader recently commented about their desire to break away from the chains that were holding them back.

I'm sharing my reply in the hope that it might inspire those who are in a similar situation to break free from their chains:

"I was in a similar situation a while back. For me it felt increasingly like being trapped in a small airtight box. I didn't know what would happen if I escaped from it, but the more I felt like I was suffocating, the more desperate I became to break out. So, while it did take courage, too, desperation was a powerful motivator. May you use it as your key and find the wondrous freedom I found on the other side of the lock."

"What Do You Know For Sure?"

$\mathcal{A}$ friend asked a great question, "What do you know for sure?"

I replied, "I know for sure that I am happiest, feel most connected, and have the greatest inner peace when I:

Count my blessings,

Know what I'm doing is making a positive difference in the world,

Am helping a friend,

Feel the love of family and friends,

View the world through kind eyes,

Experience kindness,

Am experiencing nature's beauty,

Discover something beautiful about myself or others,

See my grandsons smile, and

Share a hearty laugh with family or friends."

Casting and Attracting

A while back I read these two questions: "What are you casting out in life? What are you attracting?"

I believe that, if I know the answer to the first question, the second isn't necessary, for if I know what someone is casting out in the world I also know what they are mostly bringing in—it will largely be the same, but probably in even larger quantities.

~~~

Inner Beauty

I like to believe that the vast majority of people have inner beauty, but for many it is hidden even from themselves by materialism, pain, fear, bigotry, greed, ego, messages of scorn from others, etc. Over time, and with the help, support, and inspiration of others such as you, I believe many people will rediscover their inner beauty by pulling off the layers that have concealed it from themselves and the world.

Awakening

1 became happier than I've ever been when I began focusing less on dreaming and more on listening to my heart and spirit. Rather than reaching for the stars, I found myself already among a universe full of them.

Even One Candle

"There is not enough darkness in all the world to put out the light of even one candle."

—Robert Alden

I really like this quote. It got me to thinking about Gandhi and Martin Luther King, Jr. It occurred to me that they were both assassinated, and I asked myself, "Doesn't that mean that their lights were put out?"

That's when I realized another great truth in the quote. We can even lose our lives and still have our light live on and on.

Elegant Simplicity

Many of the ideas that matter the most are both simple and true. I said "simple" rather than "easy" because I've learned that many simple yet profound ideas are not always easy to consistently follow. Also, their very simplicity means they are often overlooked by those who believe that the world's difficult problems can only be overcome by complicated solutions.

~~~

Guilty

"You have the heart of a poet"
I was told for the longest time
And now I'm no doubt guilty
Of committing the rhyming crime.

A Bad Day's Brewin'

When I woke up
Key sites were down
Spent all mornin'
On work-arounds

Cut a toe on a tack
I didn't see on the floor
Jumped and banged my elbow
On the edge of a door

Bathroom flooded
Sewer line's blocked
Now I see I'm wearin'
Mismatched socks

Coffee pot's empty
It's plain to see
A bad day's brewin'
And it's wearin' on me

All this stuff
Is pilin' on
Everything I've touched
Has turned out wrong

But today isn't going
To get me down
It may take awhile
But I'll bring it around

Time will tell
That I was right
I'll make it a great day
If it takes all night!

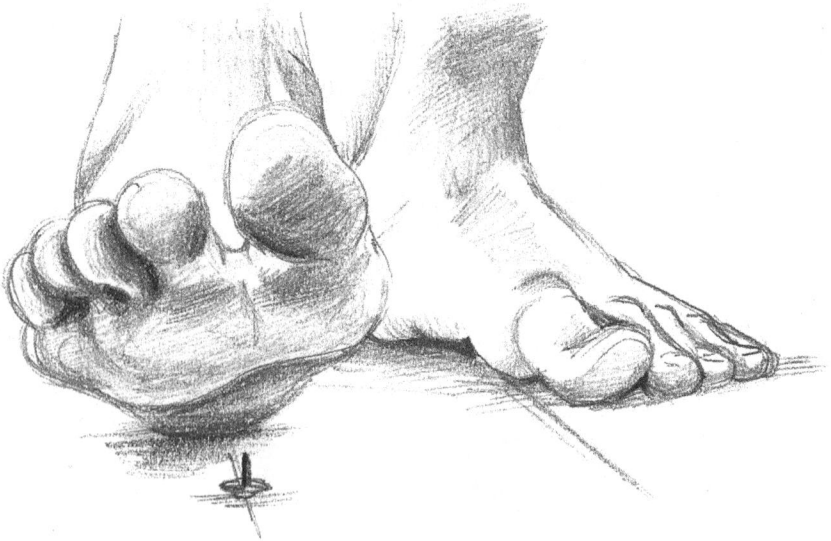

Returning the Favor

My dog, Duke, has many positive attributes, and a few that might be viewed as somewhat less than positive when I'm in a Stinking Thinking type of mood. I was about to mention a couple of the latter when it occurred to me that he is the type of friend that never, ever breaks a confidence. No matter how silly I get or how tempting that gossiping about me might be, he stays my loyal friend and keeps my foibles to himself and has never once told a tail-wagging tale at my expense.

I figured the least I could do is return the favor. So there won't be any funny stories about Duke that he wouldn't approve of—at least today. You see, while he is a nearly perfect friend, I still have much to learn from him about friendship and so many other things in life.

I'm grateful that Duke is an extraordinarily patient and forgiving teacher.

HumanKIND

I don't believe that it is a coincidence that the last four letters of the word "Humankind" spell the word "Kind." The answer to so many of our ills is even in the description of ourselves. We just need to BE kind; to BE love in action.

We already know the solution. Now, much like the need to blanket the world with inoculations against terrible diseases, we need to keep spreading the light until the darkness of apathy, neglect, greed, and violence have no place to hide and are eradicated.

~~~

My Dream

I dream of the blessed day
when humanity awakens
from its terrible nightmare
and begins to work for peace
with as much ferocity, tenacity,
and heroism as we've fought our wars.

Bliss in a Great Big Bundle of Brown Fur

I experienced sheer bliss again last night. As is often the case, I was with Duke, my chocolate lab and constant companion.

It started out as a simple trip to the grocery store to buy my wife a couple bottles of Cranberry juice. It was fairly late and I could take roads that would have little or no traffic, so I let Duke sit in his favorite "seat." He is so big that he can lie on the center console between our two front seats and, with our sunroof open, his head sticks out about six inches above the roof of the car.

Driving down the road with the look of absolute joy on his face means a lot to me. I probably have the same look on my face. I live for such moments. He and I have a bond that is indescribable and wonderful. It is great to be able to do something so easily together that brings so much joy.

It is also wonderful to see all the smiles of people who watch as we drive down the street with Duke's big ears flapping wildly in the wind.

At such moments I feel an even greater connection to Duke and all those people whom I've never even met, and all feels right with the world. I feel very blessed.

Blissful even.

For or Against

When I see news articles about people being against war, violence, poverty, drugs, crime, and many other things, I'm reminded of a brief story I heard about Mother Teresa.

During the Vietnam War, anti-war protesters invited her to join a rally against the war. She politely declined, saying something to the effect that she'd learned that it was much better to be FOR something than AGAINST anything, and that she would have accepted their invitation if it had been to participate in a rally FOR peace. (Emphasis mine.)

I believe her viewpoint was about far more than mere semantics. Mother Teresa understood that one is much more likely to have a positive and open mind when being FOR something rather than AGAINST anything.

I believe there is much power and wisdom in that concept, and I attempt to live my life accordingly.

~~~

Now is all the time I have, but if I invest it wisely, it will be enough.

It's Happening

$\mathcal{P}$rejudice is gradually being eliminated a little more every day. Certainly not in everyone. But, every time even just one person who had chosen prejudice and hate begins to choose love, acceptance, friendship and compassion instead, from that point forward their children and children's children are very likely to follow their example. When I multiply that by the number of people who are becoming less hateful and more loving every day, it gives me great hope for humankind and our planet. It isn't happening overnight, but it is happening.

The prejudice of many bigots eventually erodes when they are faced with example after example of wonderful human beings who happen to be of another race, creed, faith, tradition, etc. Sadly, some bigots will never learn, and every race, creed, faith, and tradition have their bad seeds, which are held up as examples of how awful the whole group is, but it's a game of attrition, and I believe bigotry is gradually losing ground to love and acceptance.

Will total global success occur in my lifetime? No. But I believe that progress is being made every day.

The problems are huge and daunting, but I believe in the greatness of the spirit within humankind to continue to gradually overcome them.

Do I Own My Possessions or Do They Own Me?

I believe that less is indeed often more. It is all too easy for me to get loaded with weariness when I have a lot of possessions, so I periodically ask myself this question: do I own possessions or do they own me?

There have been times in my life when I've had relatively few possessions, and, at other times, my possessions seemed to take over my life with increased clutter, greater taxes, decreased space, more paperwork, additional maintenance, etc.

Sometimes the latter got so bad that I made a rule to myself that, for every material thing I added, I needed to give away or sell something else. I used to give away whole carloads of unused items.

I now attempt to live a more frugal life with fewer material possessions but ones that I value more. To me, "Frugal" means "Not wasteful" or "Less wasteful." I find I'm happier living this way.

For example, several years ago I sold my car. I realized that, because I work at home, My Beloved and I very rarely need two cars. We've been a one-car family ever since. While it does take a little more schedule coordination, the trade-off has been a greater sense of satisfaction, lower costs, fewer taxes, more space, greater utilization of an expensive asset, and more. We have a car rental place within walking distance and it's across the street from our mechanic so, on those rare occasions when our car is in the shop, we rent a car for the day. It is still much cheaper than owning two cars.

I've often found that, when I'm feeling down, taking a little time to de-clutter an aspect of my life—something as simple as cleaning off my desk or better organizing one of our garages—often makes me feel a lot better.

~~~

1 frequently remind myself that EVERY moment is precious; once it is gone so is a part of my life that I'll never get back.

I'm working on creating a lifetime of memory-making moments.

Nature's Reminder

I believe it is no accident that the most favored flower of love in many cultures—the rose—often has big thorns along with the beauty of their exquisitely designed shape, vibrant colors, soft sensuous petals, and perfume-like scents.

I believe those thorns are a gift to remind us that even the truest loves and most joyful lives sometimes experience heartaches, disappointments, and challenges, so we will remember to appreciate all the blessings life has to offer while we can.

Avoiding a Hollow Victory

When someone tells me they are going into business for themselves, here is often my reply:

"May you find great fulfillment, satisfaction, adventure, and fun in your new venture."

I believe that when one experiences those things they are much more likely to achieve financial success, and without experiencing them, financial success will likely be a hollow victory indeed.

I've been self-employed for nearly my entire adult life in a wide variety of businesses, industries, and professions, and know firsthand the truth in both aspects of what I just said.

~~~

A Free-Range Mind

You've heard of free-range chickens or cattle. Well, the thought came to me when I was trying to focus on something detail-oriented and important today, that I have a free-range mind. It wanders all over the dang place!

A Goofy Encounter

*E*arly in our marriage, My Beloved had a little Honda Civic that seemed not much bigger than a basketball. Her personalized license plate read, "I GOOFY."

A relocation and job change ended up with my having a 3-hour and 20-minute round-trip commute, and we swapped cars to save money on gas for the long daily trips.

So, as luck would have it, "Mr. Serious" who was a shade under 6 feet tall ended up driving a motorized basketball to work with "I GOOFY" license plates. The universe sometimes has a wicked sense of humor!

I gradually became much goofier, but not much shorter!

One day, when I was driving down the highway, a woman started honking her horn at me. I couldn't figure out why. I hadn't done anything rude to her. She weaved between cars and eventually became abreast of me in the lane to my left, frantically pointing to the front and back of my car, then the front and back of her car, then back again. I still had no clue what this crazy woman was trying to communicate to me.

She then sped up slightly so that I could see the back of her car. As I looked for clues, I knew instantly what she was trying to convey. Her license plate read: "GOOFY 1."

Two goofy people had found each other and she wanted to say

"hi" and acknowledge and celebrate our shared goofiness.

A big smile spread across my face. I gave a friendly honk and a thumbs-up sign to her. She returned the gestures, and in a flash she was gone.

The memory of that moment still brings a smile to my face.

~~~

Fairy Tale Honesty

Fairy tales would be more honest (to say the least)
If they warned that sometimes Beauty IS the Beast!

Sometimes Quitting is the Right Thing to Do

1 often pride myself in not quitting, in continuing to try harder and smarter, and not giving up. That is often a smart thing to do.

But not always. I've learned the hard way that sometimes quitting is the right answer.

Sometimes a job, relationship, or situation is so awful that, even after doing everything one can to make it work, the only remaining sane option is to quit. I have been in jobs, relationships, and businesses like that.

I had a business I'd started in 1988 that had quite a number of exceptionally rewarding years. But it was a hyper-cyclical business. Despite having hundreds of clients, business could drop 95% in a month and stay at heavily reduced levels for years (such as during the dot com bust).

It was either feast or famine.

During the famine years I kept persevering, and that served me well during normal business cycles. But during the dot com bust and Great Recession—very atypical business cycles—perseverance became very harmful to our financial situation. When the economy began to improve, I was so mired in debt from trying to keep the business alive that even average years no longer produced sufficient revenue to keep the business going.

I'd been foolish to hang on so long. As I've said before, I'm a slow learner!

The flip side of the positive trait of perseverance, when taken to an extreme, is sometimes merely ego or habit-driven stubbornness.

I eventually wised up and closed the business.

That decision to quit provided the closure that I needed to begin healing financially and to move on to founding my current far-less-cyclical and much more enjoyable investment management business in 2003.

So, while I believe that in most situations quitting should be a last resort, I no longer automatically rule it out as an option.

~~~

I'll bet much more truth would transpire
If liars' pants really did catch on fire!

Empathy

When someone does something rude or unthinking in traffic, or when a child or teenager does something that brings up anger in me, or any number of other things that people have done over which I've felt anger, I've often asked myself "Have I ever done that or would I have done it if I'd led the life they've led or was having the kind of day they may be having?"

Asking myself those questions often allows me to quickly calm down and get on with my life rather than holding onto the anger. In that way, their actions no longer control my reaction, mood, attitude, view of others, or how my day is going.

Plus, I'm able to be more empathetic to the other person. I don't have to like what they did, but I can better understand why they might have done it, and forgive them for it.

It also makes it easier to forgive myself for having done such things in the past or if I do them in the future. Self-empathy can be a wonderful thing too! (I don't know if "self-empathy" is a real word, but I like it and that's good enough for me! ;-D!)

I hope your day brings a lot of good surprises to you.

~~~

I can hear the whispered wisdom of my spirit.

The Wrong Kind Of Clever

He chased fame and fortune
Grabbed both by the neck
But it's he who has been choking
As his life's become a wreck

He learned to work the system
Instead of working on himself
But lasting joy isn't found
Building that kind of wealth

A stranger lies next to him
But he knows it's not right
She'll learn the truth tomorrow
But it's haunting him tonight

He's been the wrong kind of clever
But it's not too late to change
A lifetime of habits
Chasing pleasure getting pain

He used his brain so much
He forgot he had a heart
It's time he got back in touch
With that loving part

His past is just a story
That's been keeping him down
He can write a new one
And turn himself around

Honoring a Man I've Never Met

Some time ago I went to a memorial service for a man I've never met. He was a distant relative of my elderly father-in-law who would not have been able to go if I hadn't taken him.

The deceased was born in 1918. When he was in school, his class took a bus on a field trip to a public pool to go swimming. When they arrived, he and another boy were told they couldn't go swimming and had to stay on the bus the whole time while the rest of the students got to go swimming.

They had committed a terrible crime.

They'd neglected to be born white.

He was dirt poor. So poor he had to drop out of school to help support his family. He didn't get to go to high school until he was 21—a freshman in a class full of 14-year-olds.

He joined the Army six months before Pearl Harbor was attacked. When the war began, he joined a secret unit called MIS, an intelligence group that was never mentioned in the news throughout the whole war and for a quarter of a century later. Ultimately it was credited with helping to save a million American lives and end the war two years sooner.

He served as an interpreter and interrogator to many Japanese POWs during the war, and then war criminals after Japan surrendered. He interrogated and interpreted for Tojo, Japan's Prime Minister and top war leader, and for the Japanese General who was in charge of the atrocities that occurred during the Bataan Death March.

For his wartime efforts, weeks before his death at the age of 94, he (and other remaining survivors of MIS) received the Congressional Gold Medal, America's highest award for civilians and joined the ranks of fellow recipients George Washington, Nelson Mandela, and Martin Luther King.

That memorial service was for a man I'd never met; I wish I had.

Walter Tanaka, thank you for your service and the legacy you left behind.

"Trying People"

*E*very once in a while I still catch myself saying, "I'll try." I don't want to become a "Trying" person. I want to remain a reliable one!

There are certain attributes that the people whom I most admire share. One of them is kindness. Another is that they rarely, if ever, say "I'll try."

They know words have power and tend to use phrases like "I'm on it," "It's as good as done," "You can count on me," "It's handled," or "Will do." And when they say they will do something, they very consistently do it.

Was it Yoda who said, "There is no try! There is do or do not"? I believe there is much wisdom in that concept.

One of my earliest lessons related to "trying" happened many years ago when someone in a business meeting began a sentence with "I'll try." The meeting was immediately interrupted and someone asked us all to place our pens on the table. Then they asked us to try to pick them up. As we picked them up, we were advised that we hadn't been asked to pick up the pens. We were asked to TRY to pick them up. The speaker added that we either pick up the pen or we don't, but trying doesn't belong in that sentence.

Words like "try" are mushy. They give us an out. They communicate that we think there is a good chance that we may fail. It's not exactly a confidence-building word for the people hearing it or the ones saying it.

That's why I'm focused on ridding that "try-ing" word from my vocabulary.

~~~

Clouds

Liquid smoke
Ever-changing
Ethereal and ephemeral
Whispering wisps
Bellowing billows
Drifting away

Envy

I recently had a conversation with someone who was feeling bad about his financial situation. I'll call him Trevor but that isn't his real name. Like most of us, he'd made financial mistakes and felt bad about them, especially when he compared his situation with a person (I'll call him "Fred") he knew who was about his age and far better off financially.

The thought came to me today that I wonder how things would have turned out if Fred had been born into the family, conditions, and situation that Trevor had, and vice versa. Would each have turned out like the other in this life? Would they be better off, worse off, or about the same? I believe the answer is unknowable—and that's my point.

Comparing ourselves to others is a natural thing to do, but, perhaps, not the wisest way to invest our time.

When I catch myself doing it, I tend to remind myself of some words I heard once many years ago and took to heart. They go something along these lines:

"Envy is nearly always the result of a lack of understanding of the other person's situation."

Over the years I've learned there is much wisdom and truth in those words. As with so much of what I've learned in life, I don't know who coined that phrase, how or where I heard it, or even if I've quoted it correctly, but I believe the gist of it is accurate, profound, and powerful. It has certainly helped me keep things in perspective when I've been tempted to throw a Pity-Party for myself or to gloat about how I might be "better" in some ways than someone else.

We all have burdens and we often try to do the best we can with what we've got. When I focus on this, and on counting my blessings for all that I DO have, I find that I'm much happier than when I focus on what others have or that I don't.

Speaking of envy, I've heard that of all the Seven Deadly Sins the least logical is Envy, because it is the only one where you don't get anything for it!

Life and Death, Duty and Loss

S ome time ago, My Beloved and I started our day by meeting with several family members and friends at a charity breakfast to raise funds for the Gold Star Moms organization. Gold Star Moms have all lost a child who died in service to their country, in this case in Iraq or Afghanistan. I was glad to be at the breakfast to honor and support them. It saddened me to think of the terribly high price paid by their children and the torment, sacrifice, and anguish the parents had had to deal with and were still dealing with every day. When we returned home, one of the first emails I saw was from our son, who is serving in the military. It read:

"Just saw *Act of Valor*, pretty good action flick and a decent story. There's a 'poem' at the end that I thought was very good, so I found it. The * part was left out of the movie. But I think it's good advice for life, though its subject is death."

Live your life that the fear of death can never enter your heart. Trouble no one about his religion. Respect others in their views and demand that they respect yours. Love your life, perfect your life, beautify all things in your life. Seek to make your life long and of service to your people. Prepare a noble death song for the day when you go over the great divide. Always give a word or sign of salute when meeting or passing a friend, or even a stranger, if in a lonely place. Show respect to all people, but grovel to none. When you rise in the morning, give thanks for the light, for your life, for your strength. Give thanks for your food and for the joy of living. If you see no reason to give thanks, the fault lies in yourself. *Touch not the poisonous firewater that makes wise ones turn to fools and robs the spirit of its vision.* When your time comes to die, be not like those whose hearts are filled with fear of death, so that when their time comes they weep and pray for a little more time to live their lives over again in a different way. Sing your death song, and die like a hero going home. The Teaching of Tecumseh.

I don't think it was a coincidence that, right after an event honoring people who have given more than any parent should ever have to give, I come home to a message about how to live a noble life and die a noble death.

"Live your life that the fear of death can never enter your heart." Sounds like excellent advice to me. Words to live, and die, by.

May your life be long and filled with much happiness, gratitude, love, good health, and kindness.

And may we never forget the great sacrifices made by relatively few for so many.

Ideas and Greatness

*I*t is so hard to write a truly great song that most people in the biz would much rather connect with a person capable of creating them than to try to steal rough ideas from them. It isn't altruism on their part, its pragmatism.

In many respects, stealing ideas is something that all creators do because everyone builds off the ideas, concepts, directions, and visions of others—intentionally or otherwise. Although great ideas are rare and precious, implementing them in truly great ways is infinitely harder.

One could have the idea of the statue David or the painting of the Sistine Chapel, but it takes a master to create such perfection.

I believe it was Vince Lombardi who said something to the effect that he'd have no problem sharing his playbook with the opposing team just before a game because it isn't the plays that are important but the successful execution of them.

The world is a big pie and there is plenty for everyone. People who think this way tend to recognize, appreciate, and want to play with others who think in this way, too.

Greatness can't be stolen, and ideas without greatness rarely take people very far.

Too High a Price

I was recently reminded of a saying that I like and believe is true. It is below, but I've taken some creative license with it.

"There is enough good in the worst of us and enough bad in the best of us that it behooves all of us to cut each other some slack."

I often put that concept to good use. For example, when a driver cuts me off or does something else that I consider rude, mindless, or dangerous, and I find anger or frustration building inside of me, I like to remind myself that I have sometimes done rude things while driving.

Sometimes when I've run late for an important meeting, haven't had enough sleep, was angry about something else, had to go to the bathroom, or was just plain being absent-minded, I've found myself doing the same things that I sometimes get angry at when other drivers do it "to me."

When I take a moment to think about it, in nearly all such cases, the other driver probably doesn't know or care who I am or what I think about their driving, and their actions had nothing to do with me.

Taking personal offense might be a good way to raise my blood pressure and decrease my focus on driving safely, but it's unlikely to have any impact at all on the other driver.

When I react to the behavior of others, I give away my power.

187

When I'm wise enough to remember this belief, I can shake off the anger and negative feelings and move on with my life.

When I forget to do that, I can end up in a sour mood, sometimes for quite a while—and even a minute of that is sixty seconds subtracted from my life without experiencing anything positive in exchange for it. That is too high a price for me to pay.

To See How High They Can Fly

Sometimes words start forming in my head
And that can be a good place to start
But I'm happier with what I write
When words start flowing from my heart
It's from there my spirit sings
Helps my words to have wings
Sends them soaring to the sky
See how high they can fly

~~~

I was once told by a dear friend that I say "Thank you" too often. Considering the number of the blessings in my life, I'm not convinced that I say it nearly enough!

Aglow

Aglow in gratitude
Thankful for…
…well everything
Enjoying today
And wondering
What blessings
And miracles
Tomorrow
May bring

Noticing

We've all had the kind of days when nothing seems to go right. We stub our toes, spill coffee on ourselves or someone else, get a flat tire on the way to an important meeting, accidentally hurt someone's feelings, etc. It's like a dark cloud is hovering overhead following us wherever we go.

If you are having one of those days, you have my condolences.

Fortunately, the bad days and bad times end. Sometimes it only takes a slight change of attitude or point of view.

Despite all that can go wrong, and often at the same time, we are also blessed with many moments each day that are potential unexpected pleasures although we may not be conscious of, or appreciate them, as they occur.

I have been focused on doing a better job of noticing and taking time to savor unexpected pleasures as they show up in my life: the rich golden glow of a California poppy (in the winter) when I took out the trash cans, the sound of a couple of Canada geese honking as they noisily flew by in an azure sky while I admired them through a window in my office, the swaying of trees dancing in an unusually heavy wind, the aroma of coffee or bacon in the morning, the sound of a friend's voice at the other end of the line when I answer the phone, a card or letter in the mail, the smile of a stranger, the hug of a loved one, the enthusiastic greeting of my dog when I come home, watching squirrels play hide-and-seek, and the soothing sound of splashing water.

So many unexpected pleasures happening all the time, to be experienced if only I will take the time to savor them. Much of what makes life worth living is found in such moments, if I only take the time to notice them.

My days are richer and more rewarding when I invest more time to experience, enjoy, and be grateful for, all the beauty life offers.

Simply and Magnificently "Us"

I admire the creativity of the person who created the "Coexist" graphic which is spelled out using several religious symbols. It is a clever and important message.

Coexisting is a great first step toward global peace. And, I believe that humanity has the potential to do and be so much more.

We can forgive. Share. Help and support each other. Transform from "them" and "us" to simply and magnificently "us." And, we can do it while celebrating the many ways that we are unique as well as all the ways we are the same.

What most excites me about all of this is that each of us has in our power to do, think, and feel these things right now; and in so doing, bring the world that much closer to the day when all of humanity can truly experience peace, love, and fairness, as one.

~~~

*M*y hope is that you will experience truth and kindness in my writing, and that it will remind you of the greatness and goodness within yourself and others.

That Was You?

When I was a youngster, our relatives lived out of state so my family celebrated holidays with another family in a similar situation. Virtually every house on the cul-de-sac where they lived had kids our age so we tended to go to our friends' house for the holidays.

After each holiday meal, all the kids on the block would go out to play on the well-lit, very low traffic street. There must have been twenty or thirty of us at times. Our favorite game to play after dark was Hide and Seek. The street light was "Home Base" or "Safe."

On one holiday, three sisters at a house three doors down from that of our friends challenged my two brothers and me to a game of basketball. None of the Towne boys were particularly athletic, but we were boys and were taller than them; extra height and reach is a big advantage in basketball; so we accepted the challenge. What could go wrong?

Everything. Talk about a set up! Those short girls were very athletic and very good at basketball. We got our clocks cleaned. The game wasn't even close.

Fast forward to high school. I'm an introvert and, in those days, was shy and lacked confidence with girls, especially if I had any romantic interest in them. But I was comfortable with girls who were just friends because they were "safe." I wasn't trying to get them to like me romantically so wasn't at risk emotionally with them. I didn't have to worry about the dreaded "R' word (rejection) and could just be my goofy self. I could even flirt with them a bit if they flirted with me first.

I had an upper locker and two fun and flirty girls shared a locker below mine so we used to flirt and talk to each other a lot. Their best friend was a gal who had multiple sisters and she and her sisters all looked alike to me. I didn't know how many of the sisters there were and wasn't sure of their names so I just said "hi" when I saw any of them. The girl and her sisters were in the background and I never really took much notice of any of them.

About a year after graduating from high school, I was at a party where I knew all the girls pretty well—all except one. She was sitting with a girl I knew quite well and wanted to dance with, so I politely interrupted their conversation and asked my friend for a dance. As she got up, I jokingly said to the one who was still sitting on the couch, "Don't worry, I'll have her back here shortly."

Well, I didn't. The girl and I ended up dancing for half an hour. When we were done, I remembered my joking promise to the other girl and saw that she was still sitting on the couch. I went over to her and jokingly apologized for breaking my promise and hogging her friend. She was gracious about it. I sat on the couch next to her and we began to talk.

Within minutes the strangest thing happened. We didn't talk about what people in their late teens tend to talk about. We started to talk about our dreams, and not just generic dreams, very specific ones. For example, we both wanted to have two biological children and then adopt. And the babies we wanted to adopt were some of the ones that were considered the least likely to be adoptable.

195

Those in the U.S. who were missing one or more limbs, who were blind or deaf, or had other similar challenges, or a baby from another country who was in a very bleak situation and would likely die or face terrible choices as they grew up.

It became immediately clear that we shared the same dreams; so much so that we began to finish each other's sentences as we knew what the other was going to say before we said it.

My heart sank. I was reeling. I remember thinking, "UH OH, how many girls in the whole world could possibly share my EXACT dreams? OH NO, I'm probably going to end up having to marry this girl and I don't even know her, and I don't even know whether I like her, let alone love her." I was not at all sure this was a good thing, and was completely unprepared for this situation.

I ended up asking her out for coffee after the party. My car must have been in the shop because I had my dad's Travel All (picture a huge SUV-type monster with four-wheeling off-road tires that were so big that I could barely climb into it, and she was a full foot shorter than me). And like most girls that age in those days she was wearing a short dress.

It became obvious that getting her into the vehicle was going to be kind of tricky. But she was game for it so I began to help lift/push/shove her upward. At a critical point when she was balanced precariously, I had no choice but to place my hands on her behind to finish helping her into the vehicle. But I did what was necessary to help her as any gentleman would do under the circumstances.

At the coffee shop I remember that she had lemonade and I had hot cocoa and we shared an order of onion rings. (I don't recommend having any two of those items together by the way. What were we thinking?!)

We talked for a while and when it was time to take her home I had to help her get back into my vehicle. Well, I can't say that it broke my heart. A man's gotta do what a man's gotta do.

She lived with her parents and as I turned onto her cul-de-sac memories started flooding back to me. This was the same street I'd played on as a kid on holidays for so many years. When she pointed to her house, it was the one with the basketball hoop that she and her sisters had used to massacre my brothers and me.

It became clear in an instant. I'd played Hide and Seek in the dark with her when we were young children. She gave a knowing look to me and smiled as she could see it all falling into place in my head. She'd known all along.

She kidded me about the basketball game, and about how I didn't seem to notice her at all through high school even though she was best friends and always with the two girls who had the locker below mine.

She said she'd had a crush on me all through high school. My head began to swell but I also felt bad about not noticing her sooner. Both feelings quickly disappeared when she added that she'd had a crush on a lot of boys in high school!

Six months after that fateful night we were engaged, and six months after that we were married.

Thirteen months later my Beloved Wife gave birth to the first of our two biological children, both boys. Then we adopted a little girl from Chilé.

We'd come a long way from those kids playing Hide and Seek in the dark.

And along the way we'd made our dreams come true.

To Protect His Heart

*M*y Beloved was once asked in front of a group of 50 or 60 men, "What do you believe is your most important job as a wife?"

Some of the men looked at me to see if I knew what her answer would be. I just shrugged, as I had no idea.

She replied, "To protect his heart."

She added, "It's my most important job to never break his heart."

I cherish that woman.

And, I turned the story into a poem ...

Ever Since

"What do you believe is your most important job of being a wife?"
"To protect his heart" she declared in front of fifty men that day
"My most important job is to never break his heart"
Her replies to all those guys took my breath away

My eyes overflowed with pride and love
As the men learned what I already knew
I've been one of the luckiest guys alive
Since the day she said "I do"

No Star in All the Heavens

*T*he story of the star that sits atop our tree goes back over thirty-five years. I was a young single man whose business was failing. Finances were very tight. I had enough money to buy a Christmas tree but not enough for ornaments or other decorations. A young woman who I was dating at the time saw how bare the tree looked. She made a big star out of a piece of cardboard that she'd cut out herself and then wrapped in aluminum foil that she taped to it. It sure looked good on top of my nearly-bare tree! A year later that young woman became my wife.

That star has sat in the place of honor on every Christmas tree we've had for over thirty years. During all the good years it reminds us of times when things weren't so good, and during rough years it reminds us that bad times don't last forever. But most of all, it reminds us as to how blessed we are to have the love of our family and friends.

Over the years the star became ragged-looking and has often been repaired by adding still more aluminum foil and tape. My wife sometimes suggests that we replace it with a store-bought tree-top ornament, but I can't bring myself to do it, because that star—and now that most unusual Christmas tree that so proudly holds it up— are powerful reminders of the wonderful acts of love that to me embody the true Spirit of Christmas.

No star in all the heavens is more beautiful to me than the one that sits atop our tree.

Too Stubborn and Selfish

$\mathcal{M}$y Beloved and I recently celebrated our 34th wedding anniversary, but some folks thought we'd never make it as a couple. Here is the story of one of them.

A good man who we'd asked to be the official at our wedding ceremony agreed to do so if we'd take a compatibility questionnaire. He gave it to all couples for which he officiated. We weren't fond of the idea but knew the man to be kind and if he thought it was a good idea and the information might be useful to us, then it probably would be.

So we each filled out a lengthy questionnaire and gave it to him. When the results came back, he ushered us into his office, sat us down, and in a solemn voice said something to the effect that based on our answers to the survey we were both very stubborn and selfish; so stubborn and selfish in fact that the odds of us remaining married to each other were very small.

He tried to talk us out of marrying each other, or to at least seriously considering whether marriage to each other was a good idea based on the survey's findings.

We agreed that we were both stubborn and selfish and acknowledged how that could be a huge challenge to a happy marriage, but we were in love and wanted to get married anyway.

And so we did, for we knew something that he didn't:

We were both too stubborn to ever give up on each other, and too selfish to ever let the love we had for each other slip away.

A Heart Like A Stormy Sea

He had a heart like a stormy sea
Crashing and pounding on rocky shores
Then he met her and her calm heart,
And the storm doesn't rage anymore.

My Beloved Jock and Rah-Rah

(*I* know, that is one seriously messed up title, but please hang in there with me as I hope to make it clear as to why it isn't QUITE as weird as it sounds.)

Between My Beloved and me, we have a LOT of athletic ability. Unfortunately—at least from my perspective—she is the one who has virtually ALL of it!

Back in high school, I wasn't particularly fond of some of the people who were in the groups lovingly referred to as "Jocks" and "Rah-Rahs", probably for at least two very understandable—at least from MY perspective—reasons.

1. I wasn't a Jock—not even in my dreams. For those who didn't grow up in the U.S. and may be unfamiliar with our slang, a "Jock" is a term of "endearment" given to an athlete by non-athletes, and derived from the name of the athletic supporters (also known as "cups") male athletes wear to protect critical parts of their anatomy below the waist while playing sports.

2. I had no chance in hell of ever dating a Rah-Rah. (Though in my dreams… Ahem, there goes my mind wandering off yet again. Sorry.) As I was saying, I had no chance in hell of ever dating a Rah-Rah.

In fact, I was one of THOSE guys in high school who after a girl rejected me a few times when I asked her for a date, she finally decided that she'd had enough, and told me that she couldn't go out on a date with me because she was "washing her hair." I quickly found out later that that is girl-talk which means, roughly, "No you obtuse idiot, I don't EVER want to date you, and I wouldn't date you if you were the last guy in the universe!") OUCH!

I know; I'm a SLOW learner! (But why does the world have to keep reminding me? Oh, that's right, it's because I'm a slow-learner... Sigh...)

But you know what? I had the last laugh! Despite my slightly less-than stellar athletic and dating records in high school, and my completely understandable (at least from MY perspective) dislike of some of the Jocks and Rah-Rahs, I ended up marrying both a female "Jock" and a "Rah-Rah"!

And by some miracle, 34 years later I'm STILL married to her. Who'da thunk? I guess Jocks and Rah-Rahs aren't so bad after all! ;-D!

My Beloved had been a Flag Girl, which qualifies her as being a Rah-Rah, but it was as an athlete that she REALLY shined. And in case you think I'm exaggerating, my Beloved was voted "Most Athletic" in our whole large high school.

She lettered in several sports (all that she could have lettered in due to over-lapping sports seasons), and right out of high school had even been signed to play with a newly-formed professional women's softball league! See what I mean?

Can you tell that I'm proud of Beloved's athletic abilities? What is even more amazing is that she is only 4 feet 10 inches tall (though she claims to be 4 feet 10 and ONE HALF inches tall.)

She's such a braggart! (Actually, she is humble, and isn't fond of me bringing up all of her many accomplishments, so let's just keep this our little secret, shall we? I'm the braggart, when it comes to my family and friends.)

When I say she was small, it helps to have some perspective. When I married her I believe she was only a dress size 0 or 2, and she still wears petite clothes often found in the children's section of stores. So, my Beloved was often playing against girls that were a LOT bigger than her.

Her nickname on high school sports teams was Shrimp." I still smile with pride whenever I see that name that had been sewn onto her old—okay, more like ancient—high school sweat shirt.

The position she played in softball was catcher. Girls almost twice her size and weight thought they could intimidate or bowl her over as they ran toward home plate. They were wrong.

She dug in her heals, scrunched down, and leaned into them.

The effect was not too much different than a bobcat running head-first into a bowling bowl that is sunk in concrete. Guess who most often bounced! Even the biggest girls rarely tried that twice!

By the way, my brain works in very strange ways. (As if you hadn't already noticed that a LONG time ago!) I began writing about family fun with rolled up socks—I know, that topic is strange enough by itself—but that made me think of my Beloved's amazing throwing arm, and that led me to detour onto topic.

Thank you for hanging in there when my mind runs off into its weird tangents—and titles!

Clueless

I think that most people who know me probably think that I'm a reasonably intelligent man. My Beloved knows better. Case in point:

Beloved and I got married when we were in our early 20's, and right after our wedding ceremony we received a copy of what I thought was just a cute little souvenir certificate (mistake #1) of the wedding signed by the person officiating the ceremony and our two witnesses.

In my haste to begin our honeymoon I inadvertently laid heavy luggage on top of the marriage certificate (mistake #2).

As we began unpacking at our destination, Beloved noticed the wrinkled and slightly torn marriage certificate and handed it to me. I should have taken closer notice as to the look on her face (mistake #3) and if I had, and if I'd had a functioning brain cell in my head I might have found a way to salvage the situation.

But that was not to be my fate—the lack of brains and the lack of salvaging the situation. In fact I made the situation far worse.

I know that you are probably wondering as to how anyone could be that stupid, and even if someone was that stupid, how could they make it any worse, but trust me, if a problem can be made worse I'm usually the one to find a way to do it.

As Beloved handed the mangled document to me I figured it was too far gone to be saved (mistake #4) and that we could just buy another one from the state that would have equal sentimental value to my Beloved (mistake #5), so in front of her I began to finish ripping it the rest of the way in two (Mistake # 6, 7, 8, to infinity).

As I was mid-rip, she screamed: "STOP!!! What are you doing to our marriage certificate!?!?"

That's not quite how either of us had dreamed our honeymoon would start.

If she had killed me right then, I doubt if a jury would have convicted her.

And to her credit she didn't end the marriage right then and there. Or maybe it just proves she isn't quite as bright as people think she is either!

Whatever the reason, I'm eternally grateful that she has hung in there with me for all these nearly 34 years. It hasn't always been easy, but it has rarely been boring!

And yes, we still have that original mangled 34-year old marriage certificate with a tear half way down it. It has gone through some tough times with us, but like our marriage, has always found the strength to stay together no matter what.

More Wedding Day Confessions (Sigh...)

*M*y Beloved and I were young when we got married, and we must have looked even younger than we were. I say this because when My Beloved and I decided to stop at a motel on the way to our honeymoon location the manager took one look at us and refused to book a room to us assuming we were just two young lovers using her hotel for a quick fling. This is despite the fact that we both wore wedding rings. (I guess she'd seen that ploy before.)

We didn't know where the next motel was and were completely exhausted from planning for the wedding, the wedding itself, and the reception afterwards, and I was in no mood to have to deal with the manager's efforts to attempt to protect my bride's virtue from me.

Uh oh! I just remembered another reason we were so exhausted and decided to stop there:

We'd driven many miles in the wrong direction and had to turn around and drive that many miles back.

I'd missed a turn.

But not just any old turn. Did I mention that the turn was to a SIX LANE FREEWAY with lots of highly visible signs practically shouting "TURN HERE YOU IDIOT!"?

That's how tired we were when I missed the turn. You can imagine how much more tired we were when we made the long round trip just to get back to that point. It was then that we saw the motel and knew it was time to drive no further that night.

Back to the hotel lobby: I went to Plan B and told the manager that the marriage certificate—it's the one I'd mentioned in an earlier post that I'd accidentally ripped and then like an idiot tore some more—and I'd go get it. (Plan "C" was to call the police. I was getting pretty upset at this point.)

The manager backed down and gave a room to us.

Looking back on it, some of the manager's reluctance may have been my fault. (So, what else is new?) Time for yet ANOTHER confession related to my wedding. (Sigh.)

I'd been so wrapped up in getting everything ready for the wedding that it wasn't until sometime after 6 pm on a Saturday night—the night before the wedding—that I remembered that I hadn't gotten a haircut.

And my hair was longer than it had ever been.

It had been cut military length all through high school (due to my USMC Jr. ROTC class) when nearly all the rest of the boys had long hair, so when I got out of high school I'd let it grow. And grow. With the intention of getting it cut before my wedding.

Have you ever tried getting a haircut at a barber shop at 6:30 pm on Saturday in 1979? I have, and I learned yet another lesson the hard way that night. I drove all over town and never found one that was open.

So there I was standing at the end of the aisle with hair that looked like a cross between something out of a disco movie and what you'd find on a man in a VW bus with psychedelic paint all over it.

I can just imagine what Beloved's relatives must have thought as they saw her walking down the aisle toward me. There were probably some badly bitten tongues that day!

My Beloved Makes Me
Want to Be a Better Man

I'm a lucky man. My Beloved is a teacher of Special Ed Kindergartners and First Graders and loves them. That's a good thing for me because I'm sure that she's thought on many occasions that when she comes home to me she is coming home to yet another Special Ed kid.

She has patiently stayed with this slow-learner (my words, not hers) for over thirty-four years. I can still truthfully say to her: "You make me want to be a better man" and even "You make my days better just by being in them."

As I said, I'm a lucky man.

My Wish

When I was alone and lonely, there were times I wondered whether true and lasting love was merely the stuff of fairy tales especially when my first fiancée broke off our engagement. I was heart-shattered and needed hope. I found it in the true-life stories of people who were in long-lasting committed loving relationships. I studied what they had in common and sought it in a relationship. I also looked inside myself and sought out tools and resources to help me to improve myself and my relationships. The results were well worth the effort.

It takes work and commitment to keep a relationship alive and thriving, but when it is right and the right mate is found, the return on investment is HUGE.

It is my wish that my writing about a long-term, strong, loving, and happy relationship will give hope to those who are where I was before I married My Beloved.

Acts of Love

I'm often awakened by My Beloved as she massages a special foot salve into my sometimes dry and cracked feet. When she takes care of her feet before work, she blesses me with those brief morning wake-up foot massages.

I'm grateful for such acts of love.

Water Fight!

Some of my favorite moments in life have occurred on a whim. For example, water fights between My Beloved and me. In the bathroom. They would often start innocently enough such as when I'm in the shower and she turns on hot water full blast in the bathroom sink, dropping the temperature of the water that's pouring on my shampoo-filled head to several degrees below freezing.

(OK, I know that the water wasn't frozen yet so was probably slightly above freezing, but it FELT like it was below freezing! And maybe she hadn't turned the hot water on quite full blast, but to this day I contend that was only so she could claim to be innocent while to me it looked like pretty damning evidence of premeditated malice.)

I let out an indignant bellow that could probably be heard by neighbors several blocks away, as shampoo was getting into my eyes and mouth.

And do I hear an apology from Beloved? NOOOOO. Just a little giggle. Then another, slightly louder (and to my water-clogged ears sounding a bit more taunting.)

Well, two can play at that game, so I raised the shower head over the top of the shower wall and aimed the spray right at her, drenching her clothes, hair, and everything else. Now it was her turn to shriek indignantly! And oh how she shrieked! You'd think I was killing her! I was afraid the neighbors would hear and think something nefarious was going on in our house, but I shouldn't have worried because by now they knew that some type of craziness was always going on in our house.

Being the mature woman and mother that she was, and knowing that our three impressionable young children were no doubt by now clustered on the other side of the bathroom door wondering if their parents had gone insane, she naturally and sensibly called a truce, right?

Yeah, right. She waited until I went back to rinsing the shampoo off my head, and out of my eyes and mouth, then grabbed a large glass—it must have held at least 2 or 3 gallons (well that's my side of the story and I'm sticking to it)—filled it with ice-cold water, opened the shower door, and splashed it all over me.

Then the water fight began in earnest with howls of laughter, and water drenching everything from the ceiling, drapes, towels, wallpaper, counter and fixtures, to the floor.

When we were both half-drowned and had had enough, we negotiated a truce, which takes no small amount of mutual trust in such situations as we stared each other down—me with an itchy trigger finger on the shower head, and my steely eyed foe holding two full water glasses primed for throwing.

We were both dripping from head to toe, and panting through aching jaws from laughing so hard.

We surveyed the damage we'd inflicted on our poor innocent bathroom, gave each other a knowing look, grabbed a bunch of dry towels from the closet, and began cleaning up the mess.

Such craziness is a large part of what brings the joy to us in our JOYoUS life.

1 work from home and have no commute, so My Beloved often leaves for work before I rise in the morning. That leads to a morning ritual that I love so much I wrote a poem about it:

Dream-Kiss

Asleep in our bed
So soft and warm.
A gentle touch
On my shoulder
Tells me she's there.
My head slightly lifts
Sleepy eyes barely open.
She kisses my lips
Then is gone.

How You Know

Words that form in my head
Don't do justice to how I feel
But when what I write is from my heart
That's how you know my love is real.

Focusing on the Relationship

One of the best decisions I ever made was when I decided to focus on improving my *relationships* rather than trying to improve my wife, friends, partners, children, co-workers, and others.

When I focus on the relationship, I know that it is an investment in my and our future so I don't feel resentment at the effort.

An added bonus is the other party often sees that I value the relationship with them enough to keep working to improve it. That mind-set leads to a more positive attitude within myself and quite often within the other person.

If I were to focus on their behavior, comments, or attitude it would likely lead to resistance, denial and/or resentment on their part and mine.

I work on myself, too, as I believe that is as important as focusing on the relationship. But it is when I stopped focusing on trying to fix others that my relationship with them often dramatically improved.

I've heard it put another way: "When I'm judging someone, I'm not loving them."

The Beginning of Love

The beginning of love is to let those we love be perfectly themselves, and not to twist Thoth to fit our own image. Otherwise we love only the reflection of ourselves we find in them. —Thomas Merton

I got married when I was only 21. My Beloved was only 20. I wish someone had frequently spoken the wise words above to us until we believed and followed them. Somehow—perhaps only after we had tried everything else—we came to the same conclusion as Mr. Merton. We could have saved ourselves a lot of aggravation and frustration if we had learned the wisdom of those words much earlier in our marriage.

But I'm grateful that we eventually got to that place in our marriage.

Keeping Lists

*S*ome lists make life better and some worse. I've found that grocery lists come in handy, but lists of a person's transgressions, failings, imperfections, and mistakes do not. I'm blessed to have a wife who knows that the latter type of list can be toxic to relationships. If My Beloved kept such a list about me it would be long indeed.

I believe that there *is* a kind of list that enhances relationships and our attitude toward them: "Gift Lists." They are lists of the positive attributes and actions of people. I'm not referring to the "small-g" gift lists sometimes kept as reminders of the material things people want for birthdays and other special occasions. I mean big-G Gift Lists that remind me of the many great things people bring to my life. Such Gifts are much more likely to be about the time they shared, a kindness they showed, things I enjoy about them, their positive attributes, or a fault or mistake of mine they forgot, forgave or ignored.

The most important Gifts to me almost never involve money or material things. They are far more precious because they are things money CAN'T BUY. Things like loyalty, love, trust, and true intimacy.

When I focus on such Gifts, I can't help but feel grateful and blessed.

Too Much Information

Honesty is a critical part of relationships. But there are exceptions. For example, telling a spouse your mom cooks better than they do is unwise. Fortunately despite being a slow-learner and screwing up in other ways, I never said to My Beloved that my mom is a better cook than her. I did, however, come close when I was a whole lot younger and dumber, and we were newly married.

I merely told My Beloved that a dish she cooked "tasted different" than the way my mother cooked it.

I'm surprised I survived the experience.

My Beloved wisely did what it took to make sure her silly husband never, ever, said anything like that again!

(By the way, fortunately for me, they are both good cooks.)

WAY Too Much of a Good Thing!

*O*n my wedding day, I weighed 148 pounds and stood an inch shy of six feet tall. I wasn't merely skinny, I was gaunt despite gobbling up huge amounts of nutritionally horrible and calorie-laden junk food virtually every meal of every day.

I remember eating large subway-style sandwiches with Italian meats and cheeses plus barbecue potato chips, and washing it all down with a large root beer twice per day for weeks on end.

I did add a little variety to the third meal of each day. It was usually colorful and involved dairy products: a heavily-sugared and artificially-colored kid's breakfast cereal.

If that wasn't bad enough, I worked at a donut shop where I could have all the donuts I could eat for free. I'm surprised they were able to stay in business because I was eating their profits at a pretty fast clip. (Of course, I eventually got sick of them. To this day I'm not real fond of donuts, or even their smell.)

Yeah, I know, I was a poster boy for what NOT to do nutritionally, and on many other subjects for that matter.

I could write a book about what one shouldn't do in life, and list all the things I did wrong that seemed so right at the time. Then on the last page of the book I could strongly urge readers to do the opposite of what I've done.

Good luck to the poor person who begins reading but never

finishes THAT book and then tries using it as a road map for how to live their life!

Anyway, back to my story. No matter what I ate or how many calories it contained I never gained even one measly much-needed pound. Not even an ounce.

Then I got married. To say that marriage brings on many changes is about as much of an understatement as saying that having a baby might involve an occasional loss of sleep or a slight life-style change.

My Beloved Wife cooked healthy and tasty meals. That was wonderful! A smart man would have just stuck with those meals.

I, naturally, took a different approach. I ate all those good meals and "augmented" them with the junk food to which I'd become addicted.

That combination caused me to gain weight. YAY! I gained 25 pounds and, for the first time in my life, I felt good about how much I weighed and felt I finally looked "normal." 173 pounds was perfect!

I was ecstatic! That lasted about 30 seconds as I blew right on by perfection, past pudgy, and solidly into "Oh my gosh, how in the world did I get here?" territory.

I'd gained 48 pounds. In SIX months. I gained weight so fast that I ended up with stretch marks that I still have 33 years later.

And I've been fighting the battle of the bulge ever since.

So, if you are young and single and eat a LOT of junk food, and if you have the chance to marry someone who is a good cook, be sure to think through ALL of the ramifications first! ;-D!

The Day My Beloved Got Me Fired

*B*ack in 1980, several months after we got married, my Beloved got me fired.

I had to take time off from work due to the simultaneous removal of all my wisdom teeth. I'd gotten my boss's approval for the time off in advance. Unfortunately and unbeknownst to me, at about the time that I was sitting in the oral surgeon's chair, an ugly stomach flu virus was gaining strength inside me.

When I returned home I was in pain and groggy from the surgery, anesthesia, and stitches. I'd planned to rest in bed for the rest of that day and then go back to work the next morning. It didn't work out that way.

I hadn't even made it to the bed when the symptoms of the flu hit me full force. I'll spare you the gory details, but it is probably sufficient to say that I was one very sick and miserable young man. I couldn't sleep and became very weak from making many trips between the bathroom and bed.

My Beloved called in sick for me the next morning.

When I began working at that small company, I'd heard from other employees that my boss (the owner) had the habit of calling to check to see if his employees were actually sick at home or going out on job interviews. I'd never been sick as his employee so I didn't think much of it—at least not until later that morning.

My boss telephoned and asked my Beloved to have me come to the phone. We didn't have a cordless phone in those days, and our only phone was about as far away from our bed as it could be in our modest apartment, so against her better judgment my Beloved relayed his request to me. I needed the job and thought that perhaps he needed to ask me for some important information, so I crawled out of bed and barely made it to the phone. Once he was assured that I was at home and wasn't at an interview, he abruptly ended the call, and then I dragged myself back to bed.

Shortly later, the phone rang again, and the process was repeated.

Unbelievably, a short time later, my boss called a third time. By now, I couldn't even get out of bed and was too weak to speak in any case.

My Beloved had had enough. She told him politely but firmly that I was too ill to come to the phone.

He shouted, "Look, little lady, I want you to get Russ on the phone right now!" That did it. My Beloved hardly ever swears. In fact, until then, I don't think that I'd ever heard her say an expletive that would have raised eyebrows in a holy place, but apparently she was saving up the granddaddy of all swear words for just a moment as this.

The word exploded from her mouth followed quickly by the word "YOU!" and then she hung up.

She came in to tell me what she'd done, but I'd already heard her. She was concerned that she'd gotten me fired and knew that we badly needed that income. I wanted to congratulate her for standing up to the man, but was so ill that all I could muster was a slight grin. Hopefully she saw the twinkle in my eyes that went with it. I was—and remain—very proud of her for not letting him bully her.

After he recovered a bit from the shock, he dialed our number again. She let the phone ring. Five rings. Ten. Twenty rings. Finally, she picked up the receiver and immediately placed it back on the hook.

The phone rang again. She let it ring several times, then picked up the receiver, set it on a table and walked away.

He never did get to tell her off.

Of course, I was fired as soon as I was well enough to return to the office, but that just saved me the hassle of quitting. When I recovered from my illness, I went in to the office to collect my belongings, but he'd hidden my family photos and a few other personal items in his office. I had to threaten to call the police and report the theft before he quickly returned them. Needless to say, I've never happier to leave a job than I was that day.

I learned some important lessons from that episode, including:

I needed to be more careful to be sure I had a good employer and boss.

It is best to avoid working for and with people who make my stomach churn.

My Beloved can stand up for herself—and woe be to anyone who makes her angry!

~~~

To me, love is about looking past a person's human imperfections to the beauty within their heart and spirit, and remaining focused there.

One of Us Needs to Keep Our Cool

*M*y Beloved and I learned that it can be especially bad if both of us lose our composure at the same time. We've learned that, when one of us is out of sorts, it is wise for other one to keep cool and calm until the storm has passed and not to engage while emotions are running high. That little secret has saved us from a LOT of potential arguments.

A Knock on the Door

*O*ur 25th wedding anniversary was coming soon and I wanted to honor My Beloved and celebrate our anniversary in a special way. What I had in mind was to have a few men help me surprise and serenade her. When I asked for help, I was surprised and very pleased when eleven men showed up on very short notice!

They came up with good ideas to make the experience even more memorable.

My wife heard a knock on the door and when she opened it, she was surprised to see me on one knee directly in front of her with eleven men forming a semi-circle behind me. We were each holding a long-stemmed red rose and began singing a rousing rendition of the Temptations song, "My Girl" to her. It even included some cool (or should I say "GROOVY!?") dance moves that the men had practiced at another location just prior to the knock on the door! We sang to her accompanied by a boom box playing the song.

Our audience grew as neighbors came out to see what was going on. They clapped and cheered us on.

When the song and dance were finished, each man in turn stepped forward and handed a long-stemmed red rose to My Beloved, gave her a hug and a kiss on the cheek, and congratulated her. I then gave a bouquet of 25 long-stemmed red roses—one for each year of our marriage—to her along with a big hug and kiss.

The kindness and thoughtfulness of the men helped to create a truly magical and memorable evening. While I'd known some of the men for years, I'd only recently met some of the others. They had driven up to two hours round trip in heavy commuter traffic to be there for the relatively brief experience. They all had other things that they could have been doing. Some had families waiting for them at their homes for dinner. Others took time off from work.

They weren't professional singers or performers; just regular men who gave a special gift to a special woman and me.

I'm very grateful to have My Beloved and such men in my life.

Surprise!

Sometimes, even my best intentions cause me and others all kinds of grief.

Once, I decided that it would be fun to surprise My Beloved with a new car. I came up with a reason to borrow her car, but the deal took a LOT longer to transact than I'd anticipated. I called her a couple of times to keep postponing when I was going to be home "while being out with a friend."

By the time I got home it was VERY late, hours later than I'd originally planned, and she was STEAMING. When I came through the door I sheepishly told her that "something happened to your car." At that point, my life expectancy was probably about two minutes.

Until I convinced her to go outside. There she saw her brand new car wrapped in a huge ribbon with a great big bow. On the steering wheel were a Teddy Bear and a bottle of Champagne.

It had been my turn to get a new car so she was very surprised when she got a new one before I got one.

The evening ended well ...

Keys to Our Marital Happiness

$\mathcal{A}$ friend commented something to the effect that it sounds like communication is a key part of what makes our marriage successful.

I thought I'd share my response and augment it in this post:

Yes, communication is a key part of it as is mutual respect, encouraging each other to get together with our own gender at least once per week (i.e., Girl's Night Out/Boy's Night Out—if we have a place to vent outside our home we're much less likely to feel the need to vent inside it), focusing on improving ourselves and our relationship instead of each other, shared values about all the stuff that is important to us (such as how to raise and discipline our children), agreements regarding money and budgeting (that took a LONG time to work out and was the source of a lot of disagreements over the years), knowing the minimum and maximum amount of time we should be together each week (we've learned that if we drift outside either boundary we tend to grind gears instead of mesh well together), fidelity, and trust.

They weren't listed in order of importance, just in the order I thought of them. The last two are at the end because they are so much of a given in our home that I almost forgot to list them.

I used the word "Happiness" rather than "Bliss" in the title of this post. That was accurate and intentional. Our relationship has two major imperfections: Beloved and me. (In fact, our wedding rings both contain two intentional imperfections to remind each other that we're both imperfect and will make mistakes—and that we went into the marriage fully aware of that. Our eyes were wide open. No "Love is blind" for us.)

Shared interests and hobbies weren't mentioned in the list above. While we both agree that it would be nice at times to share more interests and hobbies, we give each other the space to go our own way a lot. We tend to be loners in some ways. Heck, we don't even have similar taste in music—and I'm a lyricist!

My Beloved has ZERO interest in investing (the primary thing I do for a living), she is a big NON-fan of the types of genres I mostly write music for and has NO interest in reading what I write. Her passion for teaching Special Ed children is wonderful, but after about fifteen to thirty minutes per night of hearing what happened in her classroom, my eyes start to glaze over—as do hers when I talk about my main passions.

We'd both love it if we were enthralled with hearing the news of each other's day, but after 34 years, most such talk begins to feel like reruns. Very OLD reruns.

But we make it work pretty darn well despite the imperfections. And that reminds me as to another key to the success of our marriage:

We focus on what we LOVE about each other rather than the imperfections. Being grateful for all the wonderful qualities of our spouse goes a long way toward staying happy with each other.

In fact, I find that focusing on what I love about any situation, community, relationship, and organization goes a long way toward maintaining my own happiness.

The Dreaded Couch

$\mathcal{M}$y Beloved and I made an agreement many years ago: when we get into disagreements, whoever is the angry party and doesn't want to sleep in the same bed with their spouse is the one who sleeps on the couch.

That has saved me a LOT of being angry time because I'm about two feet too long for the couch.)

It has also been an excellent motivator to help us quickly work through our disagreements!

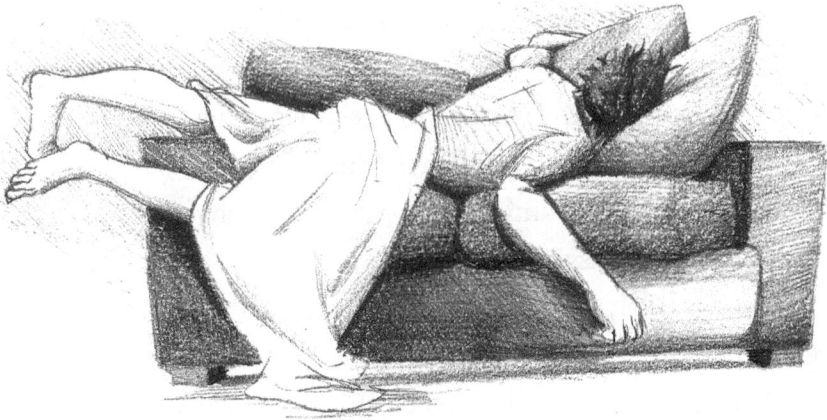

Daisy Duke and Sean Connery
Aren't Welcome at Our House

*M*y Chocolate Lab is named "Duke," which is short for "Duke of Cadbury." (I was being kind of silly when I named him but that is his name on his official registration papers.) He's plain old Duke to me.

About 3-1/2 years after Duke joined our family, My Beloved adopted Duke's half sister, a beautiful black lab pup she named Sadie. I would have preferred that she name her dog "Daisy" but, for some reason, she was not interested in having dogs that, when she called them, sounded like: "Daisy Duke! Here Daisy Duke!"

I wasn't a fan of the *Dukes of Hazzard* TV show, but I hear that the character named Daisy Duke had a LOT of male admirers... Probably every man in America has seen Daisy Duke and most of the women, too. I know for sure that at least ONE woman knows what she looked like, and that was good enough for her to avoid naming her dog Daisy.

Sometimes My Beloved just has no imagination! What a spoilsport! ;-D

Then again, knowing how much she drools when she sees Sean Connery in a movie, if My Beloved had a dog named Sean, I probably wouldn't name my dog Connery, no matter how much My Beloved begged me.

A Contest Where Everyone Wins

One Date Night, My Beloved and I were eating dinner at a restaurant that we'd never been to before. Across the way, I noticed that other tables each had huge (perhaps quart- or liter-size) coffee cups on them with various sayings. That is when I noticed one on our table, too. It read: "The one who smiles first wins!"

That's a contest I can really get into because everyone wins.

Sadie

I gave a tiny, joyful bundle of black Labrador retriever puppy fur to My Beloved as a gift. They became inseparable. As with our grand kids, My Beloved could see nothing but wonderfulness in Sadie.

In many ways, Sadie is quite a lady. She's well-behaved and a joy to be around most of the time.

But, for about the first eighteen months of her life she had a chewing problem. Actually, we were the ones with the problem. She was the one with the out-sized appetite.

Most young dogs are content chewing shoes and chew-toys. Sadie couldn't be bothered with such small things. She had her mind—and teeth—set on much larger things.

At first it was a pillow. She ripped one to pieces, eating parts of it. Then ALL of them.

When we stopped repairing and buying replacement pillows, Sadie moved onto couch cushions. That still didn't sate Sadie's voracious appetite.

Next it was the couch itself. A nibble here. A nibble there. Then the whole back panel.

We replaced the panel.

She ate the replacement.

We tried everything we could think of to get her to stop, but nothing worked.

She then began gnawing at the wooden frame inside the couch.

That was it! I'd had it. Drastic action was needed!

It was either the couch, that dog, or me!

If you know My Beloved, you know there is NO WAY it was going to be that dog.

The way I view it, our poor couch took one for the team. Yes, I put it out of its misery. I grabbed a mallet, saw, and crow bar and finished off what had become a pathetic pile of gnarled material in our living room.

Thankfully, Sadie left the rest of our furniture alone with barely a nibble here or there in the eighteen months or so since I'd said my last fond farewell to our couch.

I never did figure out what that poor couch ever did to Sadie—other than apparently being irresistibly delicious.

Who Would Do Something Silly Like That?

*T*he experience below may have been the most embarrassing day of my life—and considering how many such moments I've had, that is really saying something!

Many years ago I'd volunteered to take a carload of stuff that my employer needed for the booth of a job fair to our area's convention center. When I arrived, the road leading to the dock was long and narrow, and there was a long queue of drivers waiting to unload their vehicles one by one.

When I saw the line, I looked at my watch and sighed. Based on how slowly the line seemed to be moving, I estimated that, if I was lucky, I'd barely be able to unload, park my car, and get the booth set up in time for the stampede of thousands of job applicants waiting outside the front doors for the event to begin.

Finally, as my car reached the unloading area I saw a fellow employee on the dock signaling that if I carried the stuff from my car to him he'd relay it to the place where the booth was to be set up. Good plan!

Because it would not take long to unload the car and we were almost out of time—and in consideration of those waiting in line behind me—I left my car's engine running as I jumped out to begin unloading.

Out of habit and in my haste I locked the door as I got out.

When I went to open a rear door it wouldn't budge. Then it hit me! I'd locked my keys in my car with the engine running and a lot of people counting on me to unload and get out of their way!

I didn't quite panic yet. Thinking quickly I began to check all the doors. Maybe I'd be lucky and one would be unlocked. Nope. My heart sank as I knew right then that it was going to be THAT kind of day.

I silently screamed to myself as I sized up the potential disaster I'd just created not only for myself and my company but for everyone around me.

My adrenaline surged as I tried to figure out how I was going to get out of this mess.

I looked for a spare key in the off-chance my Beloved Wife had put one under the car and that I might have forgotten one was there.

My luck was holding. No spare key.

By now I was getting desperate and the glares of the people around me went from impatience to feelings that I'd prefer not to mention or even think about in mixed company. If looks could kill, I'd have used up more lives than a herd of cats—or is that a pride of cats?—well whatever large groups of felines are called, I was in a bad situation that was rapidly deteriorating.)

I came up with the idea to break the glass on my driver's side window, but I couldn't find anything to smash it with other than my fist or elbow. That glass suddenly looked thick and intimidating. I rationalized that I wouldn't be doing anyone any favors if I slashed an artery while shattering the window, with all of the emergency vehicles they'd have to send, etc. So, that not-so-brilliant idea was quickly scratched off my very short list of options.

I ran to the drivers of several cars who were queued up behind me and explained the situation. I don't recall their exact words at this wonderful news but between their rolling eyes and comments muttered under their breath I had a good idea that I'd just become their least favorite person on the planet, and probably the universe. If tar and feathers or a rope had been handy I think they'd have used them on me—and I can't say that I'd have blamed them.

Remember those scenes from the old westerns when the wagon train master yelled instructions and the information was shouted from one wagon to the next on down the line so that everyone would know what to do? That's about what it sounded like as I turned and raced back to my still-running car—except the tone of the modern day drivers was a LOT less friendly than the ones I remember in those movies.

I silently pleaded with my car, "Please, PLEASE don't overheat!"

People started to feverishly unload their cars and trudge the heavy equipment and boxes all along the line of vehicles as they tried to get their booths set up in time. They had to walk right by me. I apologized, but that didn't get the job done—theirs or mine.

OK, one option left, and it was a long shot. I raced to a phone (I don't remember whether we had cell phones back then but I don't think we did) and dialed my home phone number. I remembered that my Beloved Wife had planned to run errands with our two young boys that morning, so I knew that she probably wouldn't be home to answer my call. "Be home, BE HOME", my brain screamed.

After several rings, My Beloved answered. The conversation

went something like this:

Me: "Uh, honey, uh could you drop everything and bundle the kids into your car and rush down to the back of the convention center with the spare key to my car, then park your car, and with the boys in tow walk the spare keys over to me?"

Beloved: (Silence.) "Why? Did you lose your keys?"

Me: I answered, "No. I never lose my keys." I responded with my best "Who would do something silly like that?" tone in my voice. Then sheepishly said, "I locked my keys in the car..."

Beloved: "Can you wait for a while, the convention center is 40 minutes away and I'm right in the middle of..."

Me: "...with the car running. At the loading dock. With a line of cars and a bunch of angry people stuck behind me."

Beloved: "Oh..." (More silence—but this time I'm pretty sure I distinctly heard the sound of her eyes rolling.) "OK. I'll be right down..."

Have I mentioned lately how much I love that woman?

The First

She whispered, "I like you"
All the prompting I'd need
As we stood in the shade
Of a towering tree

Both new at this game
Both kind of shy
Leaned to each other
With quickly closed eyes

That bright sunny day
We shared our first kiss
She was five years old
I was barely six

Blowing the Dust Away

I was once asked: *Dust* love get dusty?

I replied: Love gets dusty …

… but investing time together, finding things to laugh about together, to be grateful for each other, to pleasantly surprise each other, hiding love notes for the other to find, treating each other as treasured best friends and not doing or saying things to each other that we wouldn't do or say to our other best friends, all have a way of blowing the dust away and replacing it with sweet moments and memories.

They Were

They were
"Committed"
To each other
Mostly
Nearly
Almost
Largely
Sort of
Partially
But one day
They realized
That commitment
Isn't a sometime
Or partial thing
It's all or nothing
And there is beauty
And strength
In commitment
When both
Are ready

Sock War!

*O*ne day when our boys were still fairly young, I kidded My Beloved about something as she sorted and matched a basket of clean socks and was rolling the matched pairs into little balls to keep them together. The next thing I knew a pair of rolled up socks was flying at me at roughly the speed of sound and hit me squarely between the eyes!

My Beloved still had her amazingly accurate throwing arm back then and she knew how to use it! She had been signed for a Pro Women's Softball League right out of high school after being voted the most athletic girl in our school. So, when I say My Beloved could throw like a pro I'm not exaggerating!

Luckily, a pair of rolled up cotton socks rolled up into a ball has not much greater impact than a, well, a cotton ball.

"Two can play that game", I yelled as I ran over and grabbed a bunch of the sock-balls from her pile then ran behind a couch and lobbed a pair at her. She ducked behind a chair with a handful of her own, and the "Sock War" was on!

By now our boys were laughing hysterically. They grabbed some sock balls, ducked behind furniture, and the war escalated.

Socks balls were flying everywhere and bouncing off of everyone and everything! We were all laughing so hard that our eyes began watering.

The cool thing about Sock Wars (besides that no one in our family ever got hurt fighting them) is that no one ever runs out of ammunition!

We played until our arms couldn't throw anymore and we'd laughed so long and hard that our jaws ached.

"Sock Wars" became one of our favorite family traditions and we often played it.

The game's only rule was that you couldn't throw dirty socks. Considering how smelly the boys and my feet were, I suspect that it was My Beloved who probably insisted on that rule!

Ironically, it was among the funnest (I know that spell-check doesn't consider "funnest" to be a real word, but if it isn't, it SHOULD be!) and funniest things we've ever done as a family, and it was FREE!

Other than the cost of an occasional re-washing of a load of socks, of course!

(I had to throw that last sentence in there just in case My Beloved reads my book!)

Date Nights

*M*y Beloved and I learned long ago that it was critical for the health of our marriage to have at least weekly Date Nights where just the two of us spend time together and at least some part of the evening is invested in talking with each other.

When we skip Date Nights, the gears of our relationship are much more likely to get out of synch and begin to grind; little irritations can become big problems, and important things are more likely to go unsaid.

Carving out time for each other helps remind us that our relationship and our spouse are important to us.

We often set aside a specific evening of the week for Date Night, but sometimes our usual night isn't ideal for one of us, so we find another night that same week that works for both of us. The important thing for our relationship is that Date Night consistently occurs nearly every week, rather than that it occurs on the exact same night each week. Flexibility, commitment, and positive attitudes help to keep our Date Nights happening and our relationship strong.

Our Date Nights can be expensive and elaborate, but often are neither. While we've found that getting out of the house is important for our Date Nights, what we do on them is less important as long as we both have an interest in or are at least open to the activities.

Since we love to eat, having dinner together tends to be one of our favorite things to do. We'll also sometimes go for a drive, go to the beach, take a walk, go to the movies, or whatever else we come up with to do together.

While we call it Date Night, our dates can be any time of the day or week. For people on a tight budget, breakfasts, lunches, and picnics can be less expensive alternatives.

We also like to have weekends together or even just a weekend day. While eating breakfast at a favorite little restaurant in the Santa Cruz Mountains one Saturday, my wife mentioned that she was exhausted from working full time and going back to college for more mandatory post-grad college courses. I suggested that we go to a nearby park so she could rest. She suggested that I buy a book so I'd have something to read while she napped. We took a couple of blankets that we keep in the trunk of the car, laid them out on a beautiful green park lawn near redwood trees and a beautiful large old historic covered bridge over a stream on a warm sunny day, and she fell asleep to the distant sounds of children playing, while I lay next to her reading a good book, watching birds soar overhead and families playing.

We were there for about three hours and it was one of our favorite recent times together.

Romance can be kept alive in many ways, and some of the best for us often involve life's simple joys and pleasures.

How Saying "I Do" Changed My Life

"*I* DO." Two of the shortest words in the English language, yet they come with the longest commitments two people can share.

I said them over 34 years ago and meant them. Thankfully, My Beloved did too—the saying and the meaning them.

It's a good thing, too, because life is full of surprises and not all of them are pleasant.

So how did saying "I do" change my life? Those two little words gave me a true life partner and friend.

We both came into the relationship with a LOT of rough edges. I was only 21 and she was a year younger. We were thrown together like rough stones into the rock tumbler of life.

We went round and round, noisily banging into each other, but always there with and for each other. In it together. Something we could count on even as life spun us. Over time we slowly ground each other's rough edges down.

While our relationship wasn't always fun and was often quite noisy, over time we both grew more polished, shined more brightly, and became a lot better for the experience.

Things will often get rocky, but it pays to keep rolling. That's the stone-cold truth that we never take for "granite."

What I Must Have

There was a time when I hadn't really thought through the relatively few things I *must have* to be happy in my relationships. The whole thing was kind of fuzzy to me. If I was asked the question on back-to-back days, the answers and the list of things would probably vary substantially and I often confused "Wants" with "Needs."

That led to frustration and unhappiness not only for me but for those poor unfortunate souls with whom I was in a relationship. If I didn't really know what I must have in a relationship, how could anyone else know what I needed?

When I finally stopped to figure out what I must have in a relationship, I was shocked to find out how hard it was for me to come up with a short and accurate list.

I learned that if an item on the list was really about the actions or inactions or attitudes of others in my relationships then it really wasn't a "Must-Have" for me. My "Must Have" list needed to be independent of the others in my relationships.

For example: "She shouldn't gossip, lie to me, cheat, drive badly" wouldn't qualify for my "Must-Have" list, but these would:

To be in a marriage in which I'm: Trusted, Respected, Appreciated ...

... and in which: My physical needs are met.

Fidelity is a given.

I've found that if I truly know what my "Must-Haves" are and if I'm getting them in my relationships, then everything else shrinks in importance and I tend to be happy, content, and fulfilled in them. I no longer really care what color paint we use, what flowers we plant, etc.

~~~

LAAF SHMILY!

My wife and I sometimes write notes or sign cards to each other that end with LAAF! and/or SHMILY! It's not because we have forgotten how to spell the words "Laugh" or "Smile." "LAAF & SHMILY" are actually acronyms for "Love Always And Forever" and "See How Much I Love You!" that we sometimes use as quick reminders that we are there for each other forevermore.

We sometimes leave notes with no other message but LAAF SHMILY where the other will find them. Such notes take very little time and, like so many of the most important things in life, are free.

Cheerios Fun with Young'uns

*M*y Beloved is a genius. She used Cheerios in various ways to raise our children. Between meals, when they were hungry, she put some Cheerios onto their high chair trays. It gave them something to do, to play with, and eat while helping them to develop their fine motor skills. It's not easy to pick up individual Cheerios lying on their sides when one is of a young high chair age.

But my favorite way she used Cheerios was when she potty-trained our boys to urinate "the way Daddy does." It became very obvious very quickly that, left to their own creativity and aim, urine would soon be all over the wall and floor—and everything in between. So, Beloved threw a couple of Cheerios in the toilet bowl to give them something to practice aiming at. It made going to the bathroom fun and quickly improved their aim.

And it encouraged Younger Son to pee into the toilet instead of into the cat litter box next to it.

As I said, My Beloved's a genius.

Every Chance I Get

Don't know what tomorrow will bring
Or even how today will end
But I know that of all of my blessings
The greatest are my family and friends.

I could live a long life or die right now
So I take every chance I get
Share all my love and gratitude
I won't live or die with regrets.

Don't Mess With Mama Raccoon!

*S*everal years ago my family went camping in a park filled with beautiful redwood trees and ferns, two of my favorite plants.

We enjoyed a pleasant, relaxing day and evening—until shortly after we tried to go to sleep. Our then-teenaged son had brought a separate small tent to sleep in, but the pole for it had gotten broken. He decided to sleep under the stars next to a large redwood tree.

He fell asleep, but soon afterwards felt a nudge. In his sleep, he dreamt that our dog was nudging him. The shaking became more insistent. He became awake enough to realize that he wasn't dreaming and something was pushing him from inside a large hole at the base of the tree!

His startled yells mixed with other screeches and noisy shuffling woke us all up. We rushed to look out the tent to see what was creating the commotion. Through blurry eyes in the near-darkness we saw our sleeping-bag-wrapped son rapidly rolling away from the tree. Then out of the hole in the tree stormed a large and very indignant mama raccoon and her babies. If looks could kill, our son would have been a goner for sure!

As the furry family scurried off into the night, we realized what had happened. Our son had inadvertently blocked their way out of the path when he had lain near the hole in the tree. His slumber had kept these nocturnal creatures from their evening meal and they were getting hungry.

That was one mad mama! She did what she had to do to make sure that her family was fed.

We eventually calmed down and had a good laugh at the pandemonium that had occurred.

Our son wisely decided to sleep in the car for the rest of the night.

It's been many years since that night, but every time my wife and I see a raccoon or a picture of one, we grin and share knowing looks.

Some memories just get better with age!

The Last Words They'll Hear

Every member of my family says "I love you" every time we leave each other, at the end of every call, and it is the last thing My Beloved and I say to each other at night.

No matter how, when, or where we die, "I love you" will be the last words the others will have heard from us.

There is something very comforting to me in that.

What I Learned from My Son and Dandelions

When our middle son was a young teenager, one of his chores was to mow the lawn. One day as I walked into the house after work, I noticed that the front yard had dandelion stems in it that were at least 6 inches tall. On top of them were the round puff-balls that blew apart on windy days. My son had promised to mow the yard the day before, but looking at those tall dandelions, it was clear that he hadn't done so.

I asked him if he had mowed the lawn the day before, and if he had, whether he did a good job. He answered yes to both questions. By now, I was getting angry.

I asked him how he could possibly have mowed the yard the day before when the dandelions were so tall today? He swore to me that he had indeed mowed the yard the day before.

I was convinced that he was lying, and children who got caught doing that in our house faced substantial consequences—often extra yard work.

My wife and I preferred to give yard work because it could be quickly completed, was not easy, and the lesson that we were trying to instill would more likely be learned and remembered.

I was about to assign a consequence to my son for lying to me, but something kept me from doing it. Perhaps it was because he didn't tend to lie. Maybe it was the earnest look in his eyes, or that he was so adamant about his innocence. Whatever the reason, I decided on a simple way to prove the truth.

I asked him to mow the yard again the next day just before I came home from work. Then when I got home I'd ensure the job was done well. The following day we'd both take a look at the lawn and if I didn't see tall dandelions with the puff balls on top I'd know that he had lied to me.

I warned him that, if the experiment proved that he was lying, the consequence would be even worse for him than if he admitted it right then. Once again he said he was telling the truth.

After work the next day, I checked the lawn and he had indeed thoroughly mowed it. There wasn't a dandelion puffball or tall stem in sight.

When I came home from work the following day I looked at the front yard. To my shock and amazement, there were many dandelion stems standing 6 inches tall. In just one day they had grown that high and sprouted puff balls!

There was now no doubt that he had been telling the truth. I felt shame for having accused him of lying to me. I asked him to come out to the front yard and sincerely apologized for falsely accusing him. I added that there was no consequence to him and that we'd do something special to make it up to him for my not trusting him when he'd given his word that he'd mowed the lawn.

My son and those dandelions taught me some important lessons that day:

I should have trusted him as I usually do.

Never underestimate either my son or nature; both can do amazing things.

Sometimes my eyes can deceive me and it is good to ask my heart for a second opinion.

A War of Wills

$\mathcal{A}$s parents, My Beloved and I were blessed with remarkably honest children. They were so honest in fact that they were downright lousy liars due to lack of practice. That often made it relatively easy for us to quickly learn the truth even during the relatively rare times they crossed that line.

Once, when our oldest son was perhaps ten to twelve years old, he took a piece of gum that wasn't his without asking. We taught our children that if you take something that isn't yours, it is stealing, and stealing is a serious matter that always has consequences.

It was only a piece of gum, but my son knew that, if he admitted taking the gum, in all likelihood he'd probably just get a reprimand or perhaps be asked to buy a pack of gum to replace it.

Instead of telling the truth, he chose to deny taking it.

It was obvious that he was lying.

My Beloved and I had taught the children from an early age that, if you break the rules, there will be a consequence, but if you lie about breaking the rules the consequences would be FAR worse than if you tell the truth right away. We then made certain that the lies ALWAYS did indeed greatly compound whatever consequences there otherwise would have been from simply breaking the rule.

He knew this and still denied that he took the gum, even after I reminded him about what happens when someone lies in our house.

Normally, he was a well-behaved child, but this time he chose a different path.

He dug in his heels and refused to admit that he took the gum. An extra chore was assigned to him. I don't recall what it was but it was most likely unpleasant and could be done in about an hour.

I came home from work the next day and he still refused to admit that he'd taken the gum, AND he had refused to do the extra chore with which he'd been tasked.

He was clearly attempting to exercise his independence. (Such times are NOT what I think of when the phrase "The joys of parenting" comes to mind!)

It was time to escalate the consequence. I reminded him that this all started with a single piece of gum, and now he had two hours' worth of yard work to do before I came home from work the next day.

The following evening, I received no confession and the yard work still hadn't been done.

I knew this was a war of wills that, as a parent, I had to win.

I took him out into our large backyard and showed him a section of what used to be a garden and was now completely filled with weeds. If I recall correctly, I told him on a Thursday night that he needed to weed a section of it on Friday.

Come Friday evening, very little weeding had been done.

I was seething. I knew that a big and important event to him was coming up that he badly wanted to participate in so I gave a final ultimatum to him:

"Weed the ENTIRE garden area (a space of about 15 feet by 50 feet) this weekend. I added for good measure, "You have until midnight Sunday to finish the job, and I don't care if you have to be out there in the dark weeding by flashlight. There better not be so much as a single blade of grass visible in that entire area or you won't be going to (whatever it was that he so badly wanted to do.)

Finally, THAT got his attention. He got up about mid-morning on Saturday and began working. He worked slowly but somewhat diligently. Unfortunately for him, when he dragged himself into the house at about dark, he was perhaps only one quarter of the way done with what had become a BIG job.

I began to feel sorry for him, but he knew I would not break my promise as to what would happen to him if he didn't meet the deadline. It wouldn't be good for him, and it would just make things harder for both of us the next time we had a war of wills. He needed to be able to count on me and my word.

He began working early on Sunday morning. His pace picked up a lot. He was clearly a young man on a mission. He worked hard for many hours and had made good progress, but as dusk approached, it was clear that he was nowhere near done.

He kept working.

He worked until it became so dark that I could no longer see him through the window.

Then, I saw a beam from a flashlight. The work continued.

I occasionally looked out the window and the flashlight beam kept moving.

Hours later, right at midnight, he came in and with an exhausted voice mumbled, "I'm done."

I sternly asked him if he got every weed and every blade of grass. He nodded yes.

The next morning, as we went out to see the job he'd done, I mentally prepared myself for seeing some missed small weeds and grass. I'd decided that if he did as good as I thought possible for someone his age, I would be prepared to cut him a little slack for the tremendous effort he'd made.

I'll never forget what I saw. The large space that had been completely covered in weeds just two days before did not have a single leaf or blade of grass anywhere on it!

I gaped at it with awe and amazement. I doubt if I could EVER have done such a good job.

I saw the pride in his eyes at the work he'd done.

I hope he saw the same in mine when I looked at him and said, "I'm proud of you for the job you did."

No truer words were ever spoken.

The Big One

I'll never forget the Loma Prieta Earthquake. Its epicenter was perhaps about 10 to 15 miles from our home.

I was working when it hit and tried to quickly get home. As I made my way down a dark expressway in very heavy traffic, I noticed something truly extraordinary. At all the major intersections that would have become badly grid locked, ordinary people had stopped, were standing in the dark in the middle of the intersection and with the help of a flashlight or flare were directing the flow of traffic.

They were risking their lives to help others. Equally wonderful was that the public responded by following their directions! The traffic was actually moving at an almost-normal pace. It was amazing! I'll never forget the kindness, consideration, and courage of those people. Because of them, I was able to get home much sooner than I expected.

I pulled into our driveway and ran into our house. It was an enormous relief to see that my family was safe. My Beloved had even had time to check on her parents who lived about 5 blocks away and they, too, were safe.

That quake had a lot of aftershocks, and some were alarmingly large. We sometimes huddled under our very sturdy dining-room table for safety. It was there, by flashlight in the dark, with the earth trembling, that I saw the photo for the first time of the miracle that was soon to be our infant daughter. The photo we'd been waiting for had finally arrived in the mail earlier that day.

I'll never forget that magical moment. We'd been waiting and working for months so that we could adopt an infant girl from Chilé. That moment sitting under our dining room table in the dark looking at her photo by flashlight was one that I'll always cherish.

Don't Smile!

*M*y Beloved and I found that one of the hardest things about disciplining our young children was staying serious when scolding them—especially when every instinct in our bodies and minds wanted to smile or burst out laughing.

For example, call us weird, but it was funny to us when one of little boys, who was potty-training, peed in the cat litter box—at least the first time he did it. (It got a LOT less funny when he kept doing it and then did it when we had guests over.) But either way, we couldn't laugh or it would spoil the lesson we needed to teach.

And sometimes, even when we couldn't laugh, we did. I know; Bad Parents!

What made it even worse is when, for example, one of us attempted to keep a straight face while explaining to the child why they shouldn't stick pudding in their sibling's ear, while our dear spouse cracked up with laughter.

We began to make up rules for each other:

"When I'm scolding a child, don't smile, giggle, snicker, laugh, or guffaw, and for goodness sake, if you are going to do those things, please do it in another room. If you won't do that, please at least stand behind the kid and do it silently so they don't see or hear you doing it!"

In our house, trying to enforce rules with our spouse tended to be more like making suggested guidelines. We are both wired in such a way that a demand or ultimatum is GUARANTEED to produce the exact opposite effect of whatever the original demanded outcome was supposed to be. We both learned it was MUCH better to request or negotiate rather than to make demands.

Back to disciplining the kids. They started getting wise to our ploy of being serious when they were facing us while their other parent (the one standing behind them) did their best to remain silent while exploding with laughter. The kids started to quickly—and without warning—turn around to try to catch the parent behind them with anything other than a serious face.

Woe to the parent who got caught!

Of course, as soon as the child turned their back on the parent who'd be standing in front of them, the roles would reverse and Ms. Smiley Pants had to be Ms. Serious, and then I could go from being Mr. Serious to Mr. Smiley Pants, or vice versa.

Now, that we're grandparents, we get to watch our adult children and their spouses go through the same thing with their children. Unfortunately, they expect us not to smile when our darling grand-children are being scolded. My Beloved and I manage to comply with such requests.

Well, at least most, er, some of the time…

Get Your Stories Straight!

Like nearly all siblings, our sons sometimes got into quarrels. When that occurred, My Beloved and I attempted to unravel how it started so we could create learning lessons as well as determine fair and appropriate consequences for their actions.

Not surprisingly, their versions of what happened sometimes differed greatly. In those situations where it was clear to us that there were no innocent victims and that they'd both broken some rules, rather than try to unravel their stories (which often created more heat than light), we found what we considered to be a fairly elegant solution.

We sent them into a room and told them that they were to stay in there until they got their stories straight and agreed on what had taken place.

Then we closed the door and waited. At first we sometimes heard continued bickering, and then silence. But usually fairly quickly, negotiations began. They realized that the length of time they'd be stuck in the room with each other, and the severity of their other consequences—if any—became completely dependent on working together to create a story that got them both off the hook.

"Well, maybe you weren't trying to hit me with the ball, and I only shoved you a little bit just kinda playing around, right?"

"Maybe you didn't eat my ice cream bar and I only thought you did, and maybe I got permission from you to eat your cookies and you just kinda forgot that you said it was okay, right?"

Once they got their stories straight, they came out and told their revised story.

It was interesting and humorous to My Beloved and me that, no matter how heated the original argument or how mistreated by the other they felt, by the time they came out of the room, they agreed the situation had mostly been one big misunderstanding or the terrible wrongs that had been inflicted on each other weren't nearly as bad as they'd originally thought.

Sometimes the stories were said with almost-gritted teeth, and sometimes they had to work through some amazing mental gymnastics to go from their original stories to the ones that they negotiated.

Sure, we knew that we probably weren't getting the whole truth and nothing but the truth, but we figured we probably weren't getting it before either and we'd only been getting their versions of the truth anyway.

At least with this "Get Your Stories Straight" strategy, they had to do the work to solve the problem—instead of My Beloved and me—and they had to work together to do it!

Besides, it was fun to hear how much their stories changed when they worked together versus when they were each trying to get the other into trouble. The hardest part for My Beloved and me was to act serious during some very humorous story changes, especially as their faces and body language contorted along with their stories.

With this approach, harmony was more quickly restored in our home.

Braces!

S ometimes it is really tough to be a kid. When both of our boys needed braces, we knew they were in for a rough time. In those days braces tended to be made out of highly visible shiny metal, and painful. We also knew that some kids would make fun of their "railroad tracks" and that could be hard on their self-esteem.

From the perspective of our sons, there was yet another big negative. The dentist gave to them a long list of chewy, gooey, wonderful things that they could not eat for the entire time they had to wear the braces, and they were warned that if they did eat the banned items they could cause permanent damage to their teeth and expensive damage to their braces.

The looks on their faces fell and stayed that way as the time for braces neared.

It hurt My Beloved and me to see them so sad, so we discussed the situation. We agreed that there wasn't much we could do about the emotional and physical pain, nor the taunting that they were likely to get at school, beyond our being open to discussing such things at whatever level the boys might feel comfortable doing so. We didn't want to "baby" them, and we wanted to support them in a healthy way.

Refraining from the goodies that were on the dentist's banned list would be hard, so we came up with an idea that we thought might at least remove some of the sting of getting braces.

A week or two before they were scheduled to get their braces, My Beloved and I sat them down and said we knew it would be tough to keep from eating all the things that were on the banned list for the whole time they wore their braces, so we were willing to make a deal with them.

We'd take them to the grocery store and let them each cram as many of their favorite items from the banned list as they could into their own large lunch bag, and then we'd let them eat it all.

We told them that we expected four things in return:

Continue to eat 3 healthy meals per day

Thoroughly brush their teeth a minimum of 3 times every day

Finish eating everything in the bag or hand over any that they hadn't eaten before the braces were put on

And they wouldn't eat any of the items on the banned list for the whole time their braces were on.

Their faces lit up as they enthusiastically agreed to the terms of our agreement so we jumped into the car and went to the grocery store with their two empty bags.

Talk about kids in a candy store! They quickly and enthusiastically filled their bags with all kinds of wonderful stuff, carefully using every millimeter of space as they scientifically jammed more of their treasure into their bulging bags.

When we got home they were thrilled with their goodies and began to enjoy their bounty. They were so happy that I think they even completely forgot about the braces for a while.

We ensured that they had healthy meals and brushed their teeth often, but otherwise left them to their goodies.

As we'd hoped, by the time their braces went on the boys were so sick of all that junk that quite a long time elapsed before they even wanted to begin to think about eating anything on the banned list again!

Hallway Torture

One of the toughest challenges My Beloved and I had as parents was regarding discipline. We wanted to be firm but loving and fair and for the consequences to be effective, age-appropriate, and child-specific.

Unfortunately, it quickly became obvious that what is a behavior-changing consequence for one child could be a nice break from routine for another.

And just about the time we found a consequence that worked for one child it tended to fairly quickly stop working for another—even when it had been working very well only a week earlier.

We also quickly learned that longer-term consequences such as "If you do that you will be grounded for a month" not only rarely deterred the behavior that we sought to avoid, it often also seemed to be more punishment for us to attempt to consistently enforce it than it was an effective post-act consequence for them.

So, we strongly preferred consequences that were quickly dealt and then done, so they—and we—could get on with life. Such consequences that were also effective were rare indeed.

We tried all sorts of things, and most weren't effective deterrents for long. That became especially true as they got older.

That is, until we discovered Hallway Torture, er, I mean Hallway Time. Our kids absolutely HATED being bored. And

274

there is nothing to do, play with, or read in our hallway. We found that if we told one of our children to sit in the hallway for a certain number of minutes as a consequence it was often a very effective deterrent indeed.

That doesn't mean that they didn't constantly try to see what they could get away with in the hallway.

They tried reading books or bringing in toys or games.

Rule change: No books, games, toys, (and if our children weren't already grown up adults and if we were parenting children today we'd definitely also prohibit all electronic devices.)

They tried hounding us with questions such as "Is the time over yet?"

Rule Change: No talking. If you talk, extra Hallway Time is added. (That backfired on us once when we forgot and a child was left in the hallway for much longer than they were supposed to. I don't recall what we did to make it up to that poor kid but I know it left them with a big smile!)

They tried sleeping.

Rule change: No sleeping. If you sleep, extra time is added. If you have to, stand up so you don't fall asleep. This isn't nap or reward time; it's consequence time.

We even found it worked for "Two-fers." When two of our children got into trouble together—especially if it was from bickering with each other—Hallway Time often worked perfectly to change the behavior.

Of course, they would try to bend the rules by whispering to each other, but we'd learned a few things by then, too.

Rules included: Be at opposite ends of the hallway; no talking, singing, or whispering; no touching/pushing/shoving or body contact of any kind. No giggling or laughing. (They would sometimes make funny faces or do silly things to try to get the other to laugh out loud and get into trouble.)

All infractions meant—you guessed it—MORE HALLWAY TIME.

We have an "L"-shaped hallway. To make it easier on our children to comply with the rules—and on us in enforcing them— we often placed the kids at opposite ends of the hallway and around the corner from each other.

Hallway Time proved to be the most effective and longest-lasting consequence for all three of our children that we ever came up with.

Your mileage may vary.

Treasure Hunt!

I collect coins that are in my pockets at the end of each day, and eventually count and roll them. When our children were fairly young, I'd keep the pennies in a big brass antique-looking container that looked like a large squat goblet with an over-sized bowl.

Rather than occasionally count and roll the pennies, My Beloved and I found a fun and educational way to deal with all of them. We asked our three young children if they'd like to go on a Treasure Hunt, and they all responded with an enthusiastic "YES!!"

So we told them we'd hidden a treasure along with a whole bunch of clues to help them find it. We said we'd give the first clue to them after they agreed to some simple rules:

Some clues were for Little Sister, some were for Younger Brother, and some were for Older Brother. Whoever the question was for must be given a few minutes to answer the question without help or hints; after that time the others can begin giving hints until the clue is found.

The clues were spread throughout our house and front and back yards, and they varied in level of difficulty for each child, and in some cases we tried to include clues to which only one of the children would know the answer. Clues might be along these lines:

Where you found the old bird's nest last month.

Where you keep the leather thing you catch balls with.

Between pages 22 and 23 of Dad's favorite book (or the book that Mom is reading.)

Underneath something that gives us light in the living room.

Wrapped around the thing we mash potatoes with.

In the pocket of your favorite shirt.

Wrapped around the handle of something we dig SMALL holes with.

It's red and you get pulled in it.

Etc.

We then provided a single clue that would lead them to another clue and so on through about 20 clues. Only the last one would lead them to the Treasure of the brass container full of pennies.

It was fun for us to come up with the clues and then watch our children work together to answer all the clues.

The kids loved the game and enjoyed dividing up their booty when at last they found their treasure.

Divide and Conquer

Much of what My Beloved and I learned about parenting was taught to us by our children. For example, if they wanted something and the first parent they asked said "no," they'd simply go to the other parent and ask again—conveniently leaving out that the other parent had already declined their request.

My Beloved and I quickly learned to ask the children if they had already asked the other parent, and if so, what the answer had been.

So, of course, the children learned to go to the Weakest Link first—who was usually My Beloved by the way. (She'd probably claim otherwise, especially when Daddy's Little Girl entered the picture.)

Since neither of us wanted to be the "Bad Guy/Gal" and there were times when we simply didn't want to make a decision or were too tired to do so, we sometimes punted. I'd say, "Go ask your mother." She'd say, "Go ask your father."

After a while, My Beloved and I realized we could be the Good Guy/Gal, by saying, "It's OK with me if it's OK with your Dad/Mom." That usually went over real well with the other parent who was stuck being the Bad Guy/Gal if "No" was the appropriate response from a mature parent....

"No, you can't have cupcakes for breakfast! What was your father thinking?!"

Which was usually quickly followed by, "RUSS! What were you

thinking saying the kids could have cupcakes for breakfast?!?!"

Kids are such tattletales sometimes!

Whenever I heard her talking to the kids about one of my "brighter" parental decisions, I often tried to make myself scarce and out of ear-shot. I had the most remarkable selective-hearing at such times—not nearly as good as that employed by our children when they were in trouble, but good nonetheless.

And our kids learned that if they were about to suffer consequences as the result of their poor decisions or behavior—as opposed to mine—they might get off easy if they could get My Beloved and me to argue regarding the appropriate consequences.

My Beloved and I learned that the best defense against that strategy was to have talked and agreed in private before approaching the child about the matter.

While our young children were master manipulators, we learned a strategy or two from them as we worked—only partially successfully—to remain firmly in charge.

When they tried to use "Divide and Conquer" to win a battle, we closed ranks and kept a united front.

We even found times when we could use "Divide and Conquer" strategies as parents.

If kids were squabbling, we'd divide them. If they were squabbling a LOT—and normal consequences weren't working—we'd sometimes each take a child for one-on-one time so that we could enjoy their presence without the terrible Sibling Squabble-Monster rearing its ugly head.

As I said, we learned much from our children—probably a lot more than they would have liked!

Parenting "Fun" with Younger Son

$\mathcal{M}$y Beloved and I are very proud of all three of our now-grown children. Each of them is unique and special in their own ways. But there were many times when pride wasn't the primary emotion we felt when dealing with them.

This post is about Younger Son when he was a child and before he became a husband, Physicist, and Captain in the USAF.

Way back then he was a:

Wannabe Cat: Shortly after learning from daddy how big boys can urinate standing up, he discovered that it was a lot more fun to pee in the cat's litter box than in the toilet—a habit he most decidedly DID NOT pick up from his daddy. He loved the sounds the kitty litter made. We had quite a time breaking him of that fun habit.

Fearless Daredevil: I once caught a glimpse of him as he began to fall head-first out of a two story window that was directly above a concrete sidewalk. I have never moved so quickly as I lunged through his bedroom and grabbed his ankles just as they moved through the window. He had stacked stuff under the window so he could reach the ledge.

Fearless Daredevil Part 2: One of Younger Sons favorite pastimes in his early years was throwing himself down a flight of stairs. He liked how he bounced and rolled. Surprisingly, he never broke a bone.

Contortionist: He once managed to squeeze his head between the railings of our staircase into a space that was so tight that we spent an hour trying to get him out. I don't remember everything we tried but I do remember salad oil and liquid dish washing soap. What a mess! I was about ready to use a saw or call the fire department when we were finally able to get his head out. I believe it was the dish washing soap that finally did the trick.

Announcer: Once when My Beloved was in a crowded grocery store he loudly exclaimed: "I have a penis, huh, mommy?" Yes, she quietly replied while trying to get him to turn down the volume several notches. He continued as loud as ever, "You don't have a penis, do you, mommy?"

Double Trouble: He and his best friend met in Kindergarten. They were inseparable, which meant that when they got into trouble they did it together.

Miner: He and Best Friend decided to dig a hole one day and worked on it for hours. They had gone down 3 or 4 feet when My Beloved decided that was deep enough. She told them it was time to fill in the hole. Later, My Beloved was impressed at how well they'd filled it in—that is until she walked onto the spot where the hole had been and the ground beneath her feet began bouncing. The little stinkers had put plywood over the hole and covered it with a thin layer of dirt so they could keep working on the hole later. They learned to regret that decision!

Construction Worker: One day Younger Son and Best Friend built a fort out of wood. It was built remarkably well for two young boys and was quite sturdy. We were proud of what they had accomplished—right up until My Beloved heard his Little Sister yelling and found they had decided it would be fun to have her go into the fort and then nail the door shut! That stunt cost them their fort and a few other consequences.

Earthquake!

Shortly after moving into our current house in 1989 I was shaken out of a deep sleep. Earthquake! And a big one!

I was disoriented from being jerked awake in the dark in a home I hadn't been in for very long. If you've ever been sleeping in dark hotel room at 3 a.m. and were abruptly awakened by a fire alarm, you know how disorienting that can be.

I quickly glanced over to make sure My Beloved wife was okay and up and moving, then began to hurry toward the bedroom of our two young boys.

Even before I reached the hallway something seemed terribly wrong. All hell seemed to break loose at once. Everything began shaking even more violently and there was a loud banging and rattling that I didn't recall hearing from prior earthquakes.

My adrenaline and fear soared when I looked down the hall into our boys' room and saw orange flickering. A terrifying thought came to me: FIRE! Oh my God, the boys!

I yelled to My Beloved and, as I raced down the hall, I kept bouncing into the walls as both they and I were swaying in the dark. I don't recall ever feeling that much panic.

A huge wave of relief swept over me as I rushed into their room as I realized that it wasn't a fire, but only their orange night light that was flickering in the dark because of the earthquake.

I ran to their beds. Our youngest son was sitting up in his bed afraid—and probably made more so by my obvious alarm. I grabbed and hugged him while looking for our older boy.

To my shock and amazement he was still sleeping soundly! Not even my yelling, the extra-loud rattling, or the quake itself woke him. (Until recently when he and his wife had their first child he could blissfully sleep through the ringing of two loud alarm clocks going off simultaneously for so long that someone else in the house had to come in and shut them off. Now, with an infant of his own to protect and care for, even small noises wake him. Welcome to fatherhood!)

The extra-noisy rattling I'd heard turned out to be a large brass ornamental spittoon with a wood and metal baton-like thing banging around inside as it was jolted around by the quake.

Soon afterward, the quake ended. Our oldest son had slept right through it. My Beloved was able to go back to sleep. Younger Son and I weren't so lucky. Our adrenaline was still pumping way too much to even consider trying to sleep.

So, we watched a funny slapstick comedy called The Great Race on TV. As we sat together, I hugged him closely and reveled in the feelings of relief and gratitude that my precious family was safe. Younger Son and I spent the whole rest of the night together, laughing and enjoying the movie and each other's company.

He is now a married man and the father of twins. To this day, any time that night is mentioned brings knowing smiles to our faces.

The Magic Touches:
A High-Five and Fist-Bump

When our children were young we were fortunate to have the option of being able to have a parent stay at home to raise our children while the other worked outside the home. My Beloved chose to focus her many talents on raising our children and I'm so glad that she did because they turned out wonderfully. She made a great full-time mom.

For the most part, I enjoyed being a part-time dad but must admit that I missed much while I was away from my family.

One day, while at the San Francisco Zoo, My Beloved took our two boys to the gorilla enclosure. A huge window separated the families of humans from those of gorillas. Our oldest son, Ben, was about four years old.

Ben was in awe of the gorillas and gently placed his little hand on the window, with his flattened palm facing them.

A giant silverback saw the gesture, walked over to the window, and gently placed his huge paw on the other side of the window exactly opposite Ben's hand. They would have been touching if not for the window barely separating them. Ben wasn't intimidated by the immense size of the powerful creature. As they stood there facing each other it was like a powerful connection was being made.

My Beloved said it was a magical moment that took her breath away. I feel the magic just writing about it decades later.

Recently, nearly 30 years after Ben's encounter with the gorilla, his son (my oldest grandson) Thomas had a very similar experience with an orangutan at the St. Louis Zoo.

The large hairy orange creature was sitting near the glass partition, and Thomas (who was only about 18 months old) toddled over to him. Thomas gently rested his fist against the glass, and the orangutan did the same. Together they made a fist-bump!

The size of the orangutan didn't intimidate Thomas at all. He'd have climbed in to play with the large hairy orange creature if the glass hadn't kept him out.

Although I missed my son's encounter with the gorilla, I was blessed to be a witness to my grandson's time with the orangutan.

The sketch is based on a photograph that Ben took of that special moment.

The Beach That Love Built

*W*hen our daughter was about 15, she was stricken with an "incurable" disease and nearly died. She spent about a month in the hospital, much of it in intensive care fighting for her life. She had to deal with an awful disease as well as many blood transfusions and the side-effects of the chemotherapy, steroids, and other harsh medications. She met each challenge, disappointment, and setback with courage and class.

Eventually, the disease went into remission and she began to dream of having a party and bonfire for her 16th birthday at the beach with her friends, relatives, and beloved dog Ginger. It took quite a bit of searching, but we finally found a beach that had all the necessary attributes including allowing dogs and bonfires, and that had easy to access for elderly relatives.

A week before her party, the disease flared up and 15 glorious months of remission ended.

Then, at 9 p.m. the night before the party, a friend called with some news that turned our plans upside down. He'd just heard that the small beach we'd selected and the surrounding beaches were about to be overwhelmed by a 30,000-person event that would essentially close them to a private party when we'd planned to be there.

The beach was out and no other beach within a reasonable

driving distance had all of the attributes required to make her dream come true.

Our daughter had her heart set on having her family and friends, dog, and a bonfire at the beach, but as usual she didn't complain. In her young life, she has had to deal with much worse things than a spoiled birthday party. But it was just the final straw on a mountain of straws that finally broke the camel's back. She sat down and quietly began to cry.

She then quickly decided that she'd rather have the party at our home so that she could at least have her dog, relatives, friends, and a bonfire. We began making the calls to invitees about the changed plans.

The next day when guests began arriving at our home (which is about 30 miles from the nearest beach) they were surprised to find a sign that read:

"Welcome to our beach, where Dogs and Bonfires are Welcome. Where the beach is small and the waves are so far away that you need to close your eyes to see them, but not the love for our daughter and her little dog, too. Happy Birthday!"

Laid out before them was the smallest, goofiest beach you ever saw, but it had been built with love. Our friends had, at a moment's notice, dreamt up creating a beach in our backyard. They had surprised us by arriving several hours earlier with a car loaded with 660 pounds of sand, a palm tree, beach toys, fish netting, Tiki Torches, and much more. Our friends and son had helped to set up everything.

The beach was built with so much love that it quickly became real to everyone there. The birthday girl and her friends frolicked in the sand, had a barbecue, built their own huge ice cream sundaes, and splashed in the water of a little pool. Then, as night fell, they lit the Tiki torches and enjoyed a great bonfire.

In the dark, by the light of the torches and bonfire, and with the splashing sounds from those playing in the water of the small wading pool in the background, the scene had indeed seemed to magically transform into a beach.

That night as the girls laughed and played on the "beach" around the bonfire with our funny little dog, I felt for a moment that all was right in the world, and was very grateful to our friends for making our daughter's birthday wish come true after all.

A Rite of Passage

$\mathcal{M}$y Beloved spent many of her formative years on a farm and knew what it was like to work hard.

I chopped firewood for my grandparents, who needed a lot of it because it was the only source of heat for their house and winters got very cold in that part of Oregon.

As the oldest of 5 children, when both my parents went to work to support us, my next-oldest sister and I ended up taking on a sizable number of chores to keep the household running. We felt like we had the whole weight of the house on our shoulders. It was far from the truth, but that is what my sister and I had thought at the time.

When My Beloved and I became adults with young kids of our own, we were concerned that, because we lived in a suburb of a large city with a stay-at-home mother, they might never truly have much opportunity to do hard physical labor and to see how much they could accomplish physically.

We wanted our children to have the opportunity to work hard and to feel good about themselves when they did.

So My Beloved and I came up with an idea. We live on a ¼-acre property and had three lawns of varying sizes that needed mowing. We had an old-fashioned human-powered push mower, and, when I judged that each child was at "about the right size," it became their responsibility to mow the lawns.

"About the right size" was when the child would have to reach up to grab the handle and had to lean into the monster with all their might to get it moving.

When I presented the "Opportunity" to each child as they reached about the right size, they were far less than enthused. They gave their best "You've GOT to be kidding, Dad!" look at me and frowned.

Their frowns didn't last long. They became scowls when they learned there was a job that they had to do before they could mow the lawn. We have dogs, and like any well-behaved self-respecting dogs they do their business outside. On our lawns.

So I handed a pooper-scooper and bag to them along with some sage fatherly advice: "It would be a very good idea to be sure to pick up ALL the mess first, because your situation will be MUCH worse if you begin mowing the lawn when it isn't."

They didn't need to be told twice.

Once they were done with that "fun" job, the real work began.

I showed them how to safely use a push mower, then let them give it a try.

They grabbed the handle with both hands and pushed. Nothing. They pushed harder. The mower began to lean in the right direction but still didn't move. Then they pushed with all their might and the mower began slowly moving.

I watched them for a while, coaching and cheering them on, then went inside while keeping an eye on them from a window.

I wanted them to be able to do it all by themselves and to know that they'd done it without help.

The job took all they had, but they gave it. I can still see the proud and exhausted looks on their faces when they finished it.

The job grew easier as they grew and developed greater mental and physical strength. About the time it became too easy for Older Son, Younger Son was "about the right size."

I took him outside, pointed to the mower, and he gave to me his best "You've GOT to be kidding, Dad!" look and frowned.

As I began to mention the job that needed to be done before he could begin mowing, I noticed out of the corner of my eye a big grin and a knowing look on Older Son's face...

Prom Nightmare

*O*ur Oldest Son had a very "memorable" Prom Night. "Memorable" as in, "Is this terrible night ever going to end?"

It had started well enough. Although he had a vehicle of his own, I'd offered to lend to him my brand-spanking new GORGEOUS car-of-my-dreams that I'd been pining over for a long time and had finally bought. To say I loved this car would almost be understatement—and there are very few material things I ever loved.

When I handed my keys to him, he knew how much faith I had in him. It was a big deal and big honor.

He was all decked out in his impressive Jr. ROTC USMC Dress Blues uniform, and had a corsage for his lovely date. As he backed out of our driveway on his way to pick her up, I mentally checked off two more rites of passage for each of us:

1. Older son going to his high school Prom

2. Older son driving my new car for the first time

He was proud and nervous. So was his dad.

When he got to the home where his date lived with her parents, there was a long narrow driveway that was squeezed between a long fence and her parents' home.

He parked, greeted her parents in the time-honored ritual that is dreaded by both the young man and the young girl's father. I have no idea what it feels like to be the young girl or her mom, but I KNOW how it is for the young man and father and let's just say it isn't high on my favorite things to do.

After everyone survived that awkward ordeal, he opened the car door for his date—he was well trained—then got in on the driver's side, and they waved goodbye to her parents.

He'd made a mental note to himself about how close he was to their house so he carefully avoided the house as he backed out. Thankfully he didn't hit their house.

He hit their fence, instead. And not just a few feet of it. A LOT of it.

He was unfamiliar with the accelerator and raced backwards quite a bit faster than he planned, turning much of their fence into splintered firewood. In front of her parents.

And, he did it not by jamming my bumper into the fence. That would have created only minor damage to my car. No, he used the whole back half of the driver's side of my car to do it. (It's funny; as I typed this I thought of the Titanic. It hit the iceberg at the worst possible angle and then dragged along much of its side doing major damage along a large length of it. That's exactly what Older Son had managed to do.)

His thoughts for a happy and fun prom night had sunk even faster than that ill-fated ship.

He got out, surveyed the damage and couldn't believe how extensive it was—to the fence and to the car. He apologized profusely to his date's parents. They were remarkably kind to him and good-natured about the whole thing. He offered to pay for the damage to their fence; then got back in what was left of my car and headed for the prom.

On a major freeway, one of the brand-new high-performance

driver's-side tires blew out. He had probably picked up a nail from the fence collision.

He got the car off the freeway and changed the tire, in his fancy dress uniform. The spare was one of those little temporary tires that look ridiculous on a car.

He finally got safely to the Prom, but I've got to believe that he was so concerned about how I would react to all the damage that I doubt he had a very good time.

When the Prom was over, he was able to get his date home safely—a minor miracle by itself considering what had gone wrong that night.

It was late when he came home. He probably hoped that I was asleep. I wasn't.

I looked out the kitchen window when he drove up. What I saw was a car that looked like it had been in a MAJOR wreck. As he got out of the car I was relieved to see that he appeared unhurt.

I noticed that my first and final reactions were exactly the same: HE'S OK. She's OK (I knew this instinctively because he'd have called me right away if anyone had gotten hurt), and IT'S ONLY A CAR..

I have to say that I was a little surprised by the latter. And relieved. And happy. And proud. It was after all, only a car. I knew then that I still had my priorities straight, and it felt good.

I think he came in steeled for the worst, and what he got was a relieved parent who calmly heard his story and said, "Don't worry about it. We'll deal with it tomorrow. Let's get some sleep."

Epilogue: He paid for half of the deductible for the car repairs, and eventually the car was as good as new.

His nightmare was finally over.

Send in the Cavalry!

As our children got into their mid to-later-teen years, they and their friends used to "hang out" a lot at our house, and usually in our living room.

It probably had a lot to do with the fact that My Beloved is a good cook and always made way too much food for our family, so our kids' friends were often invited to dinner, or to enjoy the leftovers.

I like to believe that it also had something to do with the fact that they felt safe and welcome in our home, and that they thought we were reasonably cool or OK parents and adults—or at least that we were a little less un-cool and weird then their other options.

We mostly loved that they spent so much time at our house. All of them were good kids and we knew where they were and what they were up to most of the time.

Sometimes, however, a good thing can become too much. Since they weren't old enough to go to bars, and they felt they were too old to do things like bowling or miniature golf, their options as to what to do fairly late at night became very limited.

Often—way too often—My Beloved and I heard this conversation for most of the evening:

"What do you want to do tonight?"

"I don't know, what do you want to do?"

(Repeat ad nauseam.)

They'd keep up that "conversation" for so long that it would be too late to do anything except go to a 24-hour restaurant— the SAME restaurant they'd been to every night for what seemed like months.

One night, when the monotonous conversation began, I'd had enough, and wanted to re-claim my living room from the hungry horde of bored teenagers earlier than 11 p.m..

Without saying a word I got up and picked out a cavalry movie—I love cavalry movies—and stuck it in the movie player. The next thing those teenagers heard was the sound of a bugler blowing CHARGE!

I've never seen so many teenagers clear out so fast!

Apparently they weren't fond of cavalry movies.

After that, whenever I wanted my living room back, all I had to do is ask out loud, "Now where'd I put that cavalry movie?"

Dads and Daughters

I work from home. We live in an old rural-looking neighborhood where all of the mailboxes for houses on both sides of the street are on the side that is across the street from our house. Near the mailboxes, a house was being built. Day laborers appeared to be doing much of the work.

When I went to put out the mail that morning, I noticed a car parked in front of my house with a young girl perhaps 8-10 years of age sitting in the backseat. I smiled to her when I walked back toward my house and got a beautiful, friendly smile in return. Her face lit up.

She appeared to be the daughter of one of the day workers and was most likely out of school for the Columbus Day Holiday. She was clearly in no danger as her father was keeping an attentive eye on her from across the street and the weather was beautiful. The windows were open and the temperatures were perfect so that there was no chance of her being in a car that would heat up inside to anywhere near unsafe levels.

But I felt bad for the daughter and for her father. He probably felt she was too young to leave home alone, and the construction site was way too dangerous for her to be across the street with him. So, he appeared to have done the best he could for her in a bad situation.

If I were a woman, I'd have talked to the father and invited the girl to play in our yard, perhaps even with our dogs if he approved, and if she liked.

But I am not a woman. I am a man and a father of a girl, and if I was that man and my daughter was the one in the car at that young age, I would be very concerned about a strange man being in any way attentive to her. And there is no way I'd want the man asking if my daughter could play in his yard.

But seeing that girl sitting alone in that car all morning—and who would probably be there all day—saddened me. I wanted to find some way to help relieve her boredom, to cheer her up, and to let her know that she is important, and that other people care for her well-being too.

It occurred to me that my daughter, who had just turned 23, was home and that we had a frosty bottle of root beer in our fridge. I asked her if she'd be willing to take it out to the girl and offer it to her while it was still unopened—that way the father and the girl could be assured that its contents hadn't been tampered with. I suggested she bring a bottle opener and, if the girl accepted the root beer to please open it for her so the dad could see what was going on.

My daughter agreed, and the girl accepted the soda. As this was going on I noticed that the girl's father, while still continuing to work, moved to the edge of the construction site nearest his daughter and watched without appearing to do so. It pleased me greatly to see how much he cared for his daughter and how carefully he protected her.

I was also happy that a dad and his daughter were able to find a way to show kindness to a daughter in front of her dad in a non-threatening way.

One Thing 1 Finally Got Right

I'm a slow learner in this thing called life, but there is one thing I think I've finally gotten right. I invest my time with those who, no matter how silly, strident, heart-felt, crazy, mushy, sad, stupid, childish, or whatever way I act, think, or feel, still love and accept me. That has made all the difference in my life.

Clasped Hands

*O*n a shelf near my desk are a couple of chunks of Paper Mache that I value more than if they were made of solid gold or chiseled by a master sculptor out of the finest marble.

They were made at weekend events that were created to celebrate the love of strong male relationships and to honor each other in them, as well as to help those who grieved the loss of a father, son, or brother, or were in pain from damaged, broken or non-existent relationships.

I went with my dad for one of the events, my older son for the second, and younger son for the third—the latter two when they were young adults.

Each weekend was a powerful celebration, involved forgiveness and healing, and each reinforced to me, my father, and my two sons just how blessed we were to be alive, healthy, and in strong loving relationships with each other.

During the second and third such weekend, a man introduced a process that was quite remarkable in its simplicity and quite wonderful in its result.

He asked each father and son to sit at a picnic table across from each other and clasp each other's right hand as though we were going to arm wrestle, but leave our hands upright, and then to hold that position until he said to let go.

He began to put some cloth mesh all over our hands and then slathered a thick layer of that Paper Mache goop all over the mesh covering our hands.

He then reminded us not to move, and then went to the next father/son pair to begin the process again.

At first it was a bit awkward. We were leaning toward each other with our faces only two to three feet apart and with our hands covered by a big glob of white goop—a bit out of our ordinary to say the least.

After a while of staring awkwardly, we relaxed and just started talking to each other. We were closer physically than perhaps at any time since my boys were infants or young children, other than the quick hugs that pass for physical contacts between some men of our culture.

It was intimate, and it was special. We talked and enjoyed the time with each other. When the goop on our hands solidified, the man very carefully cracked it off to keep the mold that he created intact. As we washed off our hands, he poured new Paper Mache goop into the mold we'd just made.

When the goop dried, he broke apart the mold to reveal a life-size and remarkably accurate replica of us clasping hands. Every finger, knuckle, and nail was visible.

We looked at it and knew that it was a symbol of the strength of our love and our bond and the respect we have for each other.

As I said earlier, I value those hunks of Paper Mache more than if they were made of solid gold or chiseled by a master sculptor out of the finest marble.

I see them several times per day and they often bring a smile to my face.

When my time on this planet is done, my sons will each get the one with their hand and mine.

And eventually, perhaps their children will get them, too.

How a Daunting Gauntlet
Became a Fun Zone

*S*ome years ago I was standing in a long, long line at a major theme park in southern California. I was bored, hot, and tired. I stuck a hand in my pocket and noticed that a sizable pile of coins had built up from all the change I'd received from the various park vendors.

An idea came to me that made my whole experience so much more pleasant, and even fun. I took out a quarter, and when no one was looking tossed it onto the ground near the sidewalk on which we were standing, very close to a young child. The soil softened the sound of the coin falling. The quarter shined brightly in the summer sun and sure enough the little boy saw and picked it up, excitedly exclaiming to his parents: "LOOK WHAT I FOUND!" He beamed from ear-to-ear. I smiled just as big on the inside. This was fun!

I whispered what I'd done to My Beloved so she could enjoy the experience, too. I tossed a few more coins and got similar excited reactions from other children.

The serpentine line crawled along ever-so-slowly, and we eventually got to the point where pavement was all around us, and the noise of coins hitting the hard surface would soon give me away.

I experimented and found that I could drop a coin onto the top of my shoes and the coin would roll off quietly, partially muffled by the murmuring crowd. I waited until several young children were on both sides of us in the twisting line and, as carefully and quietly as I could, I began sending coins their way. It was great to watch the children as they found and showed off their prize to their parents.

We smiled at each other. Soon, other parents started catching me as I released the coins. They just gave knowing looks to me, grinned, and didn't say a thing. One winked. It became even more fun as other parents shared our little secret. They played their part by acting surprised at the treasure that the children discovered.

If a child didn't see a coin near them, sometimes a parent would point at it and say to their youngster, "Oh look, what's that?" That's all it took to start the joyful reaction.

That simple idea was so much fun and cost so little that it was one of the best entertainment values I've ever had!

Now, long lines full of young children are opportunities rather than the daunting gauntlets they sometimes used to appear to be. They are opportunities to bring joy and smiles to young children, their parents, My Beloved, and me.

When a friend wrote that she was feeling sad and felt like her Bucket List was too rusty to hold all of her dreams, I wrote this poem to cheer her up:

Dear Friend

When you're feeling low
And the world doesn't care it seems
That your Bucket List's too rusty
To hold all your dreams
Please know you've got a friend
Who'll always believe in you
One who'd like to ease your mind
Of all the cares you're going through
Your fears, sadness, tears, and dreams
They are all safe with me
May you soon share my faith
That your dreams will become reality
I believe in your greatness
And all your goodness too
The gifts you have for the world
And most of all, I believe in you

Being There and Showing
How Much I Care

$\mathcal{A}$ while back I was asked what I did to become a better friend.

It was a lot of little things. Spoke my truth. Got more vulnerable with them and shared more of myself, my hopes, dreams, and fears, and talked to them about theirs'.

I changed my lifestyle so that I could be easily called or otherwise reached at any time of the day or night and would be available to immediately talk about 95% of the time, and for emergencies, virtually 100% of the time except the rare times when I'm flying somewhere.

I made it clear with frequent reminders that I considered it a gift and high honor when they reach out to me at the times they need me rather than when it is convenient for me—even at 3 a.m. on week nights.

Then I kept my word and followed through.

When one is easy to reach and always available, it is easier to build trust and relationships.

That approach worked with my children, too. When they became teens, I learned to be available to talk when they wanted—often between midnight and 2 a.m. or later. It kept the lines of communication open when teen hormones created a lot of interference.

I love my profession and my default mode is to be "working"

(although it often feels more like playing), but I frequently remind everyone that they are a higher priority. If they want to do something with me for fun or otherwise, almost any time of the day or night—(and if it's an emergency the word "almost" is removed)—I'm able to do it.

Much of what I do professionally can be done at any time of the day or night, so I still have plenty of time to do my duty to my Clients and meet my various responsibilities, while maintaining and enjoying relationships when it is convenient for them.

The pages of my calendar for most days are completely blank. That's exactly how I like it. My life has been designed around optimizing my availability, flexibility, and freedom.

I'm happiest when I can do what I want, the way I want, when I want to do it, while growing a business and investment portfolios, and being virtually always available for my family and friends.

A Hole in My Heart
That Wouldn't Heal

This is for all who have had someone dear to them choose to turn their back on them and walk away. If you have a hole in your heart that has never quite healed, this post is for you.

About ten years ago my best and closest friend, someone whom I'd known since second grade, completely cut me out of his life without warning. We hadn't had a fight or even a minor disagreement and I had no clue as to what I had done to cause that reaction. All attempts to find out and apologize were rebuffed.

I had a hole in my heart that wouldn't heal and my world felt out of balance.

Years later, I ran into one of his brothers and enquired as to how he was doing. His brother said he was going through a divorce, was having a very rough time of it, and could really use a friend.

I went home, picked up the phone, and tried again to reach out to my estranged friend. This time he was receptive, and our friendship resumed. I was able to be there for him when he most needed a friend.

I tell this story because it may offer hope of eventual reconciliation for some. While people are alive, hope has a chance to live on, too. And sometimes, timing is everything.

I do not know whether reconciliation will occur in your

situation(s), or even whether reconciliation is always best for everyone involved in all situations, but I do know that I wish for happiness and inner peace for you and the one(s) from whom you may be estranged, however that may look for each of you.

Far Greater than Mere Money

I have loaned quite a number of people money over the years and have always been paid back—even when the people also borrowed from others at the same time and repaid me but not the others.

When I give a loan to someone I look them in the eye and speak my truth, sometimes verbally, but most often not. There have been times when I've truthfully told others that I am giving to them the money I need for my next house payment. The loans were always repaid in time for me to pay that bill.

The look in my eyes when I give a loan to someone tells them that it isn't about the money—that it's NEVER about the money. It is about our relationship and about my belief in them as a person who keeps their word. They know that I keep my word and that I view a person's reputation, word, and integrity, as precious.

People who know me are also aware that I won't hesitate to give to them every dollar I carry in my wallet on a moment's notice. They know I don't use credit cards so I tend to have significant amounts of cash in it. They understand the reality and symbolism that I just gave them every dollar I had on my person and put their needs before my own.

When they understood the stakes were greater than mere money, they got the message and never betrayed me or our relationship.

When a Moment and a Lifetime Merge

When I was recently married and still in my early twenties, I met a woman at work who looked to me to be in her fifties and who told me a most amazing story.

She'd stopped at a traffic light when she was in her teens and a car pulled up beside her. She casually looked at the driver and he looked back at her. They'd never seen each other before.

Without either saying a word or making a motion, she pulled over and so did he.

They were married shortly later and were still happily married when I met her about 30 years later.

Sometimes people just KNOW.

That's the instant when a moment and a lifetime merge.

Perfect Moments

The longer I live
the more I become convinced
that I can either focus on
how imperfect life is
or on filling my life
with perfect moments.

"All You Need Is Love" Isn't True

*T*he Beatle's song "All You Need Is Love" is a beautiful song and I WISH it were true, but it simply isn't. At least it wasn't always true for me.

Maybe it seems that way for people who have many material possessions, but there have been times in my life where it wasn't clear where my next meal was going to come from. At that point, love and A LITTLE FOOD was all I needed.

Then, to pay for the roof over my head, love and SOME MONEY were all that I needed.

Changing the subject a bit, I've loved people who didn't love me back no matter how much love I had for them and how hard I tried to be worthy of their love or to make them love me back.

MY love wasn't all I needed. I needed THEIR love, too.

The song didn't mention that tiny, itty bitty detail.

And what about air? (I know now I'm just getting silly, but air to breathe is kind of important, doncha think?) There was a time when I had major lung problems, when I truly understood at a very visceral level just how important air is. I don't want to speak for others, so I'll say that, for these reasons, I don't believe that love is all *I* need.

But, any time I've felt without love—no matter what my financial condition—I felt very poor indeed.

And, with love I often felt much richer than a net worth statement would have shown.

So, love is MOST of what I need. But that probably wouldn't make nearly as good of a song title ...

~~~

*W*hen I was single I was not very fond of the saying, "All's fair in love and war." Perhaps it was because I was so often out-gunned!

TROUBLE!

I came from a family of seven, and when our middle names were used, we knew we were in deep trouble.

But there was another indicator that warned of even bigger problems:

When our mom REALLY got angry or flustered, she'd blank on the correct name of the child in trouble, and in her frustration she'd start running all of our names together as if it was all one name, "RussellCindyRogerRandyAnita come here NOW!!!" At that point it was almost like a military drill as we all scrambled to stand in front of her.

One of my brothers had the unfortunate trait that when he was being scolded and was especially nervous, he'd burst out laughing—which, as you might imagine, initially enraged our parents all the more. After several instances of this, they realized that he wasn't doing it to be disrespectful, and he couldn't help himself, but it made for some very unpleasant episodes for all concerned.

There were times when something bad had happened—perhaps a lamp had been broken—and we'd all be lined up. My dad or mom would ask in a stern voice, "Who broke the lamp?"

Sometimes their question would only be met by silence as we all tried to put on our most innocent "not me" faces.

After several long excruciating moments of this intense standoff, threats of dire consequences if we didn't 'fess up would begin.

If that still didn't result in a confession, the severity of the consequences would begin to escalate.

But, sometimes no one would confess despite the lengthy grilling and onerous threats. In those situations, one of my brothers would eventually often confess. I found out years later that he often confessed to things he hadn't done just because he wanted the questioning to end.

The guilty party/parties apparently had learned that if they stalled long enough they could wait him out!

Vow to a Broken Man

It took two bad lungs
And a broken heart
To finally tear
My world apart

Barely alive
In intensive care
Hoping friends would
Visit me there

Most were too busy
To visit at all
To send a card
Or bother to call

Barely able to breathe
Alone and in pain
I felt betrayed
And they were to blame

But the truth came suddenly
A cold and bitter wind
To have the love I wanted
I'd need to BE a better friend

I made a vow to the broken man
Who had 'til then been me
I'd get well and then become
The best friend that I could be

I became one who
could be counted on
No matter what the plight
From a shoulder to cry on
To help on a rainy night

Now life is so much better
I am truly blessed
For when it comes to friends
I have the very best

A Day in Paradise

$\mathcal{A}$ while back, My Beloved and I spent a day in paradise. We walked in an ancient redwood forest along a large creek with clear flowing water, small waterfalls, and deep pools. All around us towered ancient majestic redwood trees as we walked among large ferns. Redwood sorrel that looked like giant clover leafs carpeted the ground.

My Beloved, a Special Ed teacher for a mixed Kindergarten/ First Grade class, had just completed an exhausting school year the day before and badly needed a nap, so we stopped for a while in a secluded glen.

I sat on a fallen tree near the creek and My Beloved sat on the soft forest carpet leaning against me with her head resting on my chest.

The water tinkled with a soothing music that is sweeter than any wind chimes, and in no time she was asleep.

A warm but refreshing breeze gently caressed our skin as it enticed the trees to sway to the tune of the water and the wind. It looked to me as though the wind and trees were ancient dance partners swaying to a primal song, ever changing yet ever the same.

The sun and shadows were not to be outdone as they danced among the trees and plants and on the forest floor. I thought their dance seemed a bit hurried, perhaps because they knew that, when darkness fell at the end of the day, their fun would end until morning, but the wind and trees could continue dancing and playing all night. I wondered if the sun and shadows cursed the unfairness of it all.

Our secret glen was full of spirit and magic and majesty.

As I sat in reverence to the awesome beauty all around, my senses came alive with the sounds of the wind and water, the rough feel of the fallen tree and the softness of the wind, and the smells of the forest that are so unique and pure and earthy.

Watching the water do its own dance among the stones in the stream brought me back to the many times as a child my friends and siblings would race leaves or twigs on the surface of creeks. Or just sit and watch in curiosity and amazement as water skeeters raced along in calmer sections of the stream.

For a while, I was a child again.

As I sat there in reverie, my back, behind, arms, and legs began to ache as I tried not to move to avoid waking My Beloved—my body reminding me that while my mind can be any age, my body sometimes has other needs and ideas.

But an even stronger feeling came to me as I sat in silence letting the soothing rhythms of nature refresh my spirit in that glorious masterpiece of nature, with the woman of my life in my arms: This wasn't merely paradise.

This was *home*.

Terror and Kindness on Interstate 5

*I*t was the middle of the night on one of those long and lonely stretches of Interstate 5 between distant small farming communities. My mom and her girlfriend were taking me and four other children to Disneyland. All eight of us were jammed into our Travel-All, a large SUV-type vehicle that had huge and heavy tires that were made for 4-wheeling.

Suddenly our vehicle began wobbling wildly, as if the big beast was trying to decide whether to flip over sideways or end-over-end! We started spinning while bucking violently from side to side. A kaleidoscope of zigzagging, spinning lights streaked all around us as we grabbed in sheer terror for something to hang onto as we braced for the inevitable crash or roll.

Time seemed to slow to a crawl while our world spun out of control in a never-ending fast-motion nightmare. As we stopped spinning, we were hit with a shockwave of blaring horns and the glaring lights of two rapidly approaching eighteen-wheelers. Our dazed brains came to the realization that we were straddling both lanes while facing the wrong way on the freeway!

There was no time to react or to get out of the way. We watched in sheer terror as the big rigs roared past just inches away from each side of us. Our Travel-All shook, but I don't know whether it was from the trucks rocketing past so close or from our trembling nerves.

We limped off to the side of the highway. It was very dark, but it was clear that both a front and rear tire that were diagonally opposite each other had blown nearly simultaneously. We were lucky to be alive!

But, we remained in a dangerous situation stuck on the side of the freeway with one spare tire and two flats in the dark with traffic whizzing by.

A man driving a big rig stopped, sized up our predicament, and offered to take one of us to the nearest town where he knew someone he could call who could help us. I could tell that our moms didn't want to leave the little kids, nor be alone with a strange man on a dark highway, miles away from anyone, so, as the oldest child it was up to me to go. I was scared, too, but my going with him seemed the best option.

As it turns out, I was in good hands. The trucker got me safely to his friend's shop, woke him, and he worked several hours through the night to get us back on the road again.

I'll never forget the kindness and consideration shown by those men. It would have been much easier for the trucker to ignore us and to keep to his schedule, and for the shop owner to say, "Sorry we're closed until tomorrow morning," but they both chose a different way—and that made all the difference for two moms and a truckload of impressionable kids who learned some valuable lessons about the huge difference kindness can make in the lives of others.

Rusty

When I was in the hospital recovering from lung surgery many years ago, a friend gave a teddy bear to me. He knew that I'd long outgrown such gifts, but seeing how miserable, drugged-up and helpless I was, he decided a teddy bear was symbolically appropriate and might just provide some comfort. It did, and I appreciated the gesture.

The bear was rust-colored, so I called it Rusty. It may also have had something to do with the fact that, as a little boy, my nickname was Rusty. I was named after the little boy's character in a television show called Rin-Tin-Tin.

Rusty was with me in the hospital and in the long, painful weeks during my recovery at home.

Later, when I married and when we began having children, my family learned how Rusty had been with me throughout my illness. When one of us got sick, Rusty was there to help comfort them. It wasn't long before our young children began bringing Rusty to whoever was sick "to help them get better."

Rusty is now over 36 years old. He has faithfully been there for everyone in my family many times. His presence is not only comforting, but a symbol of our love.

Rusty has been through a lot with us. Over the years he has become tattered. He is not much to look at anymore, but you should see the appreciative grin on the face of whoever is ill when he is brought to them.

Our children are now all adults. As they marry and have families of their own, I have no doubt that such a tradition will continue with a stuffed animal for their families.

In the meantime, Rusty is still here, faithfully and lovingly waiting to help comfort any grandchildren who visit.

I P O Y

I occasionally write the letters "I P O Y" on the bottom of emails and other written communications to one of my sons. The reason for doing so takes a little explaining but involves Fred Rogers of "Mr. Roger's Neighborhood" fame...

I never knew much about Fred Rogers until one of my sons sent an audio-book chronicling the author's friendship over the years with Fred Rogers. I don't recall the name of the book (unless it was "IPOY") but it had a lasting impression on me.

I was impressed that how Fred Rogers projected himself in his television show is very much like he was in real life: kind, gentle, compassionate, thoughtful, loving, and understanding—in life and during his painful illness, and tragic death. He was clearly a man whose words and actions were in alignment with his vision and purpose.

I never watched his children's show for more than a few minutes as I flipped through TV channels, but even in those brief moments of curiosity I saw a man who was willing to be ridiculed by many adults as he created a safe space for young children to bring their fears and anxieties and be comforted and befriended as they became more confident and comfortable about themselves and their world.

In the audio-book, the writer was dealing with some troubling things from his childhood that were having a major negative impact on his life as an adult. Though Fred Rogers had barely met and didn't know him, Fred reached out and quickly became a close and trusted friend, confidant, and life-and-relationship coach to him despite the fact that, during most of the time of their friendship, they lived far apart. Most of their communications were via letter. The book appears to be largely based on those letters.

One of the issues the author struggled with was around self-worth. Fred began writing "I P O Y" at the bottom of many of his letters to the author. It was their short-hand for "I'm Proud Of You." That simple lesson in kindness greatly touched the author and had a major impact on his life.

And that is why to this day I occasionally write those four little letters at the bottom of my written communications to the son who sent the audio-book to me. I am indeed proud of him and all three of my children, and it is nice to have a way to remind him of that in a special way.

I hope it brings a smile to his face when he sees "I P O Y" and remembers a kind and gentle man who made the world a better place while he was here.

All the Way

Going "All the way" sexually
Heck, that's the easy part
Compared to
What it takes
To follow through
In matters of the heart

A Dying Man's Last Request

*M*y biological father was an avid golfer. He always dreamed of playing the Pebble Beach Golf Course. He and another man wanted to play the course together, so they began to pool their savings in a big 5-gallon bottle kept at the other man's house. When the bottle was full and they could afford to go, his "friend" took all the money and spent it.

My biological father, who lived on the East Coast, never got to fulfill his dream.

When he died, his wife told me after he had passed that his last request was that I would scatter his ashes on the Pebble Beach Golf Course.

GULP! Something that you may not know about me is that I tend to be a Rule Follower, and if I don't like someone else's rules I tend to change games—which is one reason I'm self-employed (my game, my rules)—but this request definitely fit into the Rule Breaker side of things. I figured that, if I fulfilled his last request, I would certainly be breaking several rules and, most likely, several laws.

I was torn. Badly.

Ultimately, blood proved thicker than mere rules and laws (and I have probably never in my life used the word "mere" in front of either of the words "rules" and "laws").

I discussed my dilemma with My Beloved. She was no happier

or comfortable with the request than I, and probably much less so, but she offered to come along to offer moral support. We both knew there was a chance that I would be caught and arrested, and if she was with me she could suffer a similar fate, but she wanted to come anyway, and woe be to the person who tries to tell her "no" when she sets her mind to something.

When the day came, we drove to Pebble Beach, becoming more anxious with each mile closer we'd gotten, too nervous to even enjoy the fantastic views on the way there.

We noted with growing concern that security vehicles and guards were everywhere. It's like they had their own private army.

We scoped the perimeter like a couple on a secret mission. Actually, we were a couple on a secret mission. Piercing the perimeter looked like a really BAD idea.

Our nerves were on edge but we also noticed that along with the risk and "danger" an element of excitement and adventure began to creep in.

The theme song from the original Mission Impossible TV show kept running through my head. Seriously.

My Beloved put the clay urn full of ashes in her purse as we parked our car. We walked through the magnificent clubhouse with its main room that is so large that it has two HUGE and very impressive fireplaces.

The view was magnificent! We walked out the back of the clubhouse, across a patio with diners, down some steps and onto a large lawn area that led out to a stone edge, which marked the end of the lawn and the beginning of a small beach several feet below and the Monterey Bay.

The golf course's 18th hole was to our left and near the stone wall. I don't recall what separated the course from the lawn near the stone edge but it wasn't much of an obstacle. Perhaps a rope.

We had much bigger obstacles to deal with. First, parties of golfers were very often either on the green making their final putts or on their way to it. I couldn't just waltz onto it and start spreading ashes all over it.

But the biggest obstacle was that a security guard must have decided that we looked suspicious and began following us onto the long beautiful green lawn that gently sloped down toward the Bay.

Our hearts raced as we looked at each other, wondering what to do. We'd come too far to turn back now. In a whisper I suggested that we sit on the on the edge of the lawn at the rock edge right up against the 18th hole and try to look like sightseers.

The security guard hung back and off to our right about 20-25 feet and appeared to be cleaning his nails. Yeah, right!

I decided to lie down parallel to the golf course and up against it with my back facing the guard. My Beloved took out her camera and pretended to take pictures, gradually moving her body into a position that would perfectly obstruct the guard's view. She reached into her purse and handed the urn to me. I placed it in front of me and covered it with a jacket.

But it became obvious that there was no way I was going to be able to walk onto the green without immediately drawing attention to myself, being stopped, and possibly arrested.

We did catch a lucky break in that a strong wind was blowing inland from the Bay, so if I could time the space between the golf parties just right, and if I could throw the ashes into the wind without being seen by golfers on the course, people in the clubhouse, diners on the patio, and the ever-present and attentive guard, the ashes would float onto the 18th green.

There were too many "IFs" for my taste, but it was the hand we'd been dealt so we'd try to play it.

The whole urn and ashes thing had kind of creeped me out, so I hadn't opened the lid of the clay urn since it had been handed to me on the East Coast.

That proved to be a BIG mistake!

When I think of ashes, I think of those soft floaty things that gently float up from a campfire. So, when I reached into the urn I expected to feel kind of a soft, light powder.

My eyes must have gotten huge when I felt nothing even remotely resembling ashes!

It felt like a nearly solid mass with a consistency that was closer to sandstone than ashes. (It should be noted here that I was aware that what I was touching was the last physical remains of the man who was one of two humans responsible for bringing me into this world and that his remains should be treated with respect.)

Still, I was freaked out. It might have even been funny under other circumstances but, at the moment, laughter was about the furthest thing from my mind as I felt a surge of panic.

I groaned, then whispered the latest problem to My Beloved. She gave a startled expression followed by a shrug and a, "Well I guess you're just going to have to deal with it" look that I knew so well.

But it was My Beloved who came up with the next tactic, whispering "I'll distract the guard" as she picked up the camera and walked away.

I looked over my shoulder following her with my eyes and watching the guard out of my peripheral vision as I began feverishly scraping the contents of the urn with my fingernails, trying to loosen it all.

I waited for that hoped-for critical moment when everything aligned perfectly: The 18th green had no one on or near it, the guard was facing away, and the wind was gusting in from the Bay. I just had to hope that no one else walked onto the lawn and that everyone else was too far away to notice what I was up to.

The seconds turned to minutes, dragging on interminably, while I continued scraping the contents of the urn as My Beloved continued slowly walking to the other side of the lawn, pretending to take photos of the gorgeous scenery.

The guard had the choice of watching My Beloved to his right, turning his back on me, or vice versa. He chose her. GOOD CHOICE!

Just then the 18th green was clear, and I slowly and nonchalantly stretched my right arm high over onto the golf course as if I were stretching contentedly without a care in the world. As I did so I opened my hand and flicked the contents with my fingers. To my great relief and with substantial help from the wind they scattered over the 18th green. I did this several more times, never knowing if the next toss would end with my arrest, but lucking out every time.

I signaled to My Beloved when I was done, and we reversed the process, getting everything back into her purse.

As I stood up I felt as though a huge weight had been lifted from my shoulders. MISSION ACCOMPLISHED!

The two successful secret agents soaked in our success, and even took a victory lap of sorts. We walked into the clubhouse and sat in some beautiful chairs. I ordered my biological father's favorite drink, a Dirty Vodka Martini on the rocks, and My Beloved ordered a glass of champagne.

We toasted him.

Then we toasted what we'd accomplished together.

I don't recall ever having a drink that I enjoyed more.

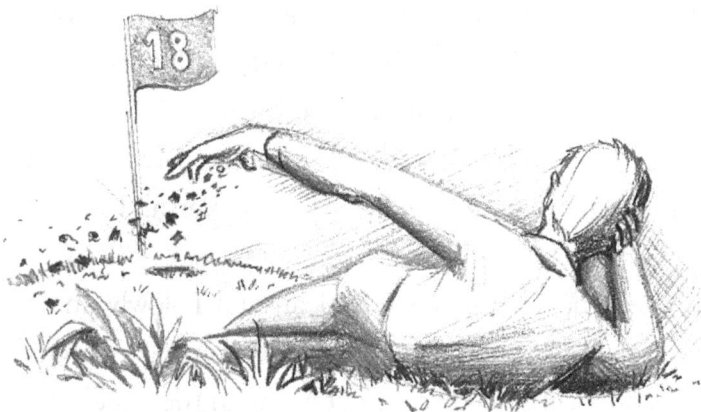

Under One Roof: Twelve Kids, Two Women, and One Very Patient Man

When I was in my early- to mid-teens a maternal aunt and her seven children moved in with our family of seven into a three-bedroom/two-bathroom house. They were from the east coast and none of the kids from each family knew those from the opposite coast.

The five boys were in one bedroom and the seven girls in another. Thank goodness for bunk beds with three mattresses! Personal space was rare and precious, and privacy was a wonderful concept with virtually no chance of reality.

Despite major efforts by everyone, I'm sure that noise levels greatly exceeded volume standards for jet engines. That must have been very tough on the nerves of the adults.

Certain aspects of life needed to be fairly tightly regimented. For example, with fifteen people and only two bathrooms, you can imagine how crazy that got! The lines could get as bad as those at a ball game at half-time. And, there was often more dancing and squirming while standing in those lines than what might be seen at a high school dance.

The ambiance at meal time was akin to a military mess hall with a platoon of hungry recruits devouring everything in sight. In our house it was be fast or go hungry.

It took multiple shopping carts piled as high as possible just to keep food on the table. I can't even imagine how much it cost to feed all of us!

And the piles of laundry were mountainous and never-ending. Our clothes washer and dryer worked around the clock.

The older kids helped around the house—though I'm sure that we didn't help nearly as much as we thought we did, or as the adults would have liked! I was the oldest of the twelve kids and I was still fairly young.

Schedules needed to be strictly adhered to. One person running late could wreak havoc on everyone, and getting everyone out of the house on time resembled a cross between a fire drill and a scene from the Keystone Cops—but with a LOT more noise.

While all this might seem to be a recipe for disaster or misery, I don't remember it that way. We had a whole bunch of cousins we hadn't known before to get to know and to play with.

We all just kept finding ways to make it work.

It must have been tough for my mom and her sister to live under one roof with each other and so many children, but I can't even imagine how it must have been for my poor Dad.

Bob Fukuda

$\mathcal{M}$y father-in-law is a quiet man, and a good one. I've been blessed to have had him in my life for over 34 years. He's a quiet and humble man who just does what needs doing when it needs doing. That's my definition of a hero.

I recently told Bob how much he has meant to me and my family and how much I've enjoyed and appreciated having him as my father-in-law.

He simply replied, "Well, I don't talk much" with an embarrassed shrug, but the look in his eyes told me he was touched by the sincere compliments.

Duke

I thought of my dog Duke when typing about kindness. When I'm sick in bed he quietly lies next to me, keeping me warm and watching over me, never leaving my side—a quiet watchful sentinel.

I work from home and Duke loves to stay under my desk, his muzzle resting on my feet. It is nice to have his company. With him I'm never alone.

I'm blessed with good friends, and Duke is one of the best.

He's not perfect. He has flaws like me. But he forgives mine, and I try to return the favor every chance I get.

Genesis: This started as a poem about my dog Duke and turned into a lyric for a song honoring the deep bond of love between many people and their dogs.

My Old Friend

You picked me the moment we met
And you knew right from the start
We were supposed to be together
You ran straight to my arms and into my heart.
I couldn't ask for a more loyal companion
You'd risk your life to save mine.
When I was sick in bed for a week
You stayed right by my side the whole time.
You once ruined our brand new carpet
When you ate my whole birthday cake.
My wife forgave us because you're cute
Though getting sick is no excuse for the mess you made!

But I'm far from perfect too
I can be cranky for days
When I growl 'n bark and snap at you
You still always love me anyways.

Your face is growing whiter and your pace is off a step
Let's make the most of whatever time we have left.

My Old Friend,
Life with you is better, My Old Friend
It's always an adventure I wish would never end,
And I'm glad we have each other, My Old Friend!
So glad we have each other, My Old Friend.

Home Maintenance

Our lawns need mowing
A cobweb's growing
A gate is sagging
Repairs are lagging
Shelves are dusty
A latch is rusty
A faucet leaks
Our hall floor creaks
Laundry's piled on the floor
A broken knob is on a door
Our housekeeping is far from kept
But our home's well maintained in some respects
The work we do around our house
Is less on things and more on ourselves
Love and laughter are brightly shined
And we focus on being kind
We don't skimp on telling the truth
But for lies we have no use
Ego corrodes so we remove it fast
That's how we make relationships last

Our home's foundation is built on trust
With big strong beams that'll never rust
Our home is warmed with love all night
And lit all day with love's bright light
Our joy and fun have a brilliant gleam
Trust and faith has a polished sheen
Folks would do well to go somewhere else
If they want to visit a clean house
But if love and friendship are what you prefer
That kind of maintenance we don't defer
So come in friends enjoy your stay
May you feel welcome every day

I wrote this poem shortly after my first grandson was born, to honor him and to remind me as to what can happen if I ever forget how it feels to see the world through the eyes of a child.

Silly, Silly Me

He grabbed my hand and yelled, "Come see! Come see!"
And excitedly pointed to our big shade tree.
"Yes I see; it's a tree" I thoughtlessly said.
With wise young eyes, he shook his head.
"Silly Grandpa, Can't you see?
It's not just a tree! It's so much more.
It's a place to play, to build, to climb, and explore
A secret place to talk and hide
Or to pretend that we're real spies!
Now it was my turn to shake my head
"Silly, silly me! Of course!" I said.
"How could I have forgotten?
It's much more than a tree!
The years had blinded these old eyes
To all the things a tree can be.
Thank goodness you were here
To help me once again see!'

"Grandpa, come see what else I've found!
It's big, light brown, and on the ground. "
Slow learner that I am, I said to him:
"It's the box our refrigerator came in."
"Silly Grandpa," he sighed and said, "Can't you see?
It's not just a box; it's ANYTHING we want it to be!
A great big castle with a moat
A pirate ship or ranger boat
A fire engine that fights huge fires
Or a Monster Truck with great big tires.
A real fast car that we can race
Or a rocket ship in outer space.
A screaming jet that we can fly
Or a helicopter up real high
It can even be a submarine
See? It can be anything!"
I then remembered a thing or three
About what a cardboard box can be
I shared ideas that I recalled
He smiled and said, "Grandpa,
You're not so silly after all!"

This poem is dedicated to Brian and Kristi, parents of our twin baby grandsons.

The Race

Moving in slow motion
Can hardly think at all
Vision's getting fuzzy
Movements slowing to a crawl
Forgot to leave the porch light on
Can't fit my key in the lock
Tell myself I need more sleep
As I fumble in the dark
It's a slow-motion race
As I stagger through the door
For my head to hit my pillow
Before my face hits the floor.

Family Nights

*P*icture if you will all the noise and people during rush hour in Grand Central Station, the commotion and energy of a busy dog park, the love and joy of a raucous religious revival, the laughter and entertainment of a circus, and a meal fit for a king but large enough to feed an army, and you begin to have some idea as to what it is like to be at our house on most Sunday evenings.

That's because we celebrate Family Night on Sundays, and all of the above is usually generated by just my immediate family. And our dogs. Six dogs. (Our adult children bring their dogs so they can play while we do.)

It's also a bit like a mini United Nations (without all the rancor, bickering, and squabbling) as my immediate family represents races from three continents.

If I ever needed a reminder as to how much abundance and love is in my life, Family Night would serve that purpose.

Family Nights now include three and sometimes four generations, as our grandchildren have entered the world, and my in-laws are also sometimes able to join us.

Speaking of our grandson, he has of course become the star of the show. Even our wonderfully entertaining dogs all enthusiastically playing together can't compete with this latest attraction.

We also often have a conference call with our son who is a

Captain in the U.S. Air Force and stationed in Illinois and his delightful wife. They recently gave TWIN grandsons to us! YAHOOOOO!

Family Nights are one of my favorite experiences of the week. In the midst of all the noise and activity, I often sit back and soak it all in, savoring every second of our time together, feeling incredibly grateful to be blessed having so many wonderful people in my life who know all my faults and love me anyway.

When No One Else Was

Thank you
To all who
Were there with love
When no one else was
—Or would have been
Had you known me then.

~~~

As my heart has grown so has my world.

The Sweetest Words of All

I've had lots of roles and titles
But of the many things I've been called
"Husband", "Dad", and "Grandpa"
Are the sweetest of them all!

About the Author

$\mathcal{R}$ uss Towne lives in the San Francisco Bay Area with his wife of 34 years, Heidi. They have three adult children, and three grandsons including a pair of twins.

Russ manages the investments of the wealth management firm he founded in 2003.

Convinced he didn't have a creative bone in his body, at the age of 52 a friend invited him to co-write a song. Russ loved the process, and quickly co-wrote several songs, wrote over 100 poems, and began writing non-fiction and children's books.